NEWBIE'S GUIDE TO SELLING FACE-TO-FACE

QUICK START FOR CONSULTANTS, FREELANCERS, NEW SELF-EMPLOYED, CAREER CHANGERS, START-UPS

Michael McGaulley

Copyright © 2010-2021, Michael McGaulley.

All rights reserved. Michael McGaulley and Champlain House Media.

ISBN-13: 978-1544861982

ISBN-10: 1544861982

ASIN: B06XCR1K6Q

No part of this book, whether delivered electronically (e-book) or in conventional paper form (p-book), may be reproduced or transmitted in any form by any means graphic, electronic, or mechanical without the written permission from the author, Michael McGaulley, the publisher, or affiliated companies.

Legal information, including additional copyright data and legal disclaimers, are at the end of this book. Your proceeding beyond this point indicates acceptance of these policies.

This is a revised and updated replacement of an earlier book, **How to Sell Face-to-Face Survival Guide**, by the same author.

Note: This book**, Newbie's *Guide to Selling-Face-to-Face,*** is what the title implies: a book particularly useful as a starter guide for people new to selling, or going off in their own, such as new start-up entrepreneurs, new consultants, new free-agents and free-lancers.

I have purposely kept it as short and to-the-point as possible so the "newbies" can get on with it without having to sort out what is need to know for them from the more advanced how-to appropriate for experienced sales people.

If you are among the latter, looking for more in-depth how-to selling skills training and techniques, I suggest my other books, which you will find at the back of this book. Or check the website at:

www.   Sales-Training-Source.com

TABLE OF CONTENTS

PREFACE _____ 1

Step 1: QUESTIONS FOR FOCUSING YOURSELF, YOUR BUSINESS CONCEPT, AND YOUR APPROACH _____ 9

Step 2: DEVELOPING A LIST OF POTENTIAL PROSPECTS _____ 21

Step 3: FINDING YOUR WAY TO THE "PROSPECT"—THAT IS, THE PERSON OR TEAM WHO CAN SAY YES _____ 27

Step 4: INITIATING YOUR FIRST CONTACT _____ 35

Step 5: GETTING PAST THE GATE-KEEPER _____ 39

Step 6: MAKING YOUR FIRST PHONE CONTACT WITH THE PROSPECT _____ 47

Step 7: PREPARING FOR YOUR FIRST FACE-TO-FACE WITH THE PROSPECT _____ 53

Step 8: OPENING YOUR FIRST FACE-TO-FACE WITH THIS PROSPECT 59

Step 9: WORKING WITH THE PROSPECT TO UNCOVER NEEDS FOR WHAT YOU OFFER _____ 67

Step 10: CONSULTATIVE SELLING: SELL BY ASKING SMART QUESTIONS _____ 73

Step 11: MAKING CLEAR THE LINK BETWEEN THE PROSPECT'S NEEDS AND HOW YOUR PRODUCT (OR SERVICE) WILL FILL THOSE NEEDS __ 85

Step 12: WHEN DEALING WITH THE ISSUE OF PRICE, FOCUS ON "VALUE" _____ 93

Step 13: BEING ATTUNED TO "BUYING SIGNALS" _____ 103

Step 14: CLOSING FOR THE ORDER, OR FOR OTHER TYPES OF "BUYING ACTION" _____ 111

Step 15: **RESPONDING TO OBJECTIONS AND QUESTIONS** _____ *121*

Step 16: **AFTER THE SALE: CUSTOMER CARE, AND FOLLOW-UP** ___ *131*

ABOUT THE AUTHOR/OTHER BOOKS _____ *137*

PREFACE

Are you beginning a career in sales? A small-business person? Starting up a new venture? Going out on your own? Free agent? Independent contractor? Consultant? In career transition and looking for a new job or a new field?

"If you can sell, you'll always eat."

Good advice from a relative of mine, William McGaulley, drawn from his experiences as a young guy working his way across the country and back during the Great Depression of the 1930's.

We're a long way from the kind of the kind of tough economy he faced back then, but his advice is still as sound as ever. People who can sell— whether they sell ideas, products, services, or expertise, or even sell themselves in job interviews— live better and gain control of their lives and destinies.

"But I can't sell! I'm just not a sales-type, and never will be!"

Chances are you said much the same thing when you were a kid: "I can't ride a bike, I just can't!"

But you tried it, you persisted, you learned the skills, you got rolling, you built confidence . . . and now riding a bike is second-nature to you.

Learning to sell will be the same.

Michael McGaulley

"Selling is not in my job-description"

Well, maybe it needs to be in your job-description . . . whatever that job is, and especially if you don't currently have a job.

In my work as a management consultant, I met a lot of talented people who were failing to live up to their true potential. The single most common reason, I found, was that they had never learned to "sell" . . . that is, to sell themselves and their ideas and capabilities — to people "upstairs."

My point? Selling within an organization is not that different than being an outsider selling to an organization. You can adapt most of the ideas in this book to selling yourself within your job, whatever that job may be.

And if you've lost your job, or if you're coming out of school looking for work? Then it's very wise to make selling part of the job-description you create for yourself.

On that note, see *USA Today*, "Today's MBA graduates create their own jobs." (April 27, 2009)

The point was this: in other years, graduates tended to be recruited for jobs in Wall Street banks and investment houses, consulting firms, and the like.

But now, in part because of the recession and resulting job cutbacks, in part because of personal choice, more and more of the new graduates are looking into starting their own ventures.

That's a great idea.

But . . .

The but is that they will soon find that, even if they are CEO of their own company, they still need to sell—sell to prospective users, sell to suppliers that may be reluctant to sell to start-ups, sell to potential investors, sell to landlords who may be reluctant to rent space to new ventures. and sell to new employees . . . and sell to others.

In the real world, "free-agents" don't have agents

The kind of free-agents we're speaking of here are not out-of-work ballplayers looking for their next multi-million dollar contract with the help of their millionaire sports agent/negotiators.

The reality is that free-agents are a very significant and growing force in today's job marketplace. In an article in *USA Today*, columnist Laura Vanderkam (herself a free-agent) turned up these figures:

- 26% of U.S. workers are now free agents, up from 19% in 2006.

- In New York City, the comptroller found that self-employment accounted for 491,000 of the 773,000 jobs the city gained during the "fat years" of 1981 to 2006.

- Though not all free agents had gone into free agency as a voluntary choice, about three-quarters planned to remain free (free agents, that is).

- Free-agency may become even more the way of the future as projects are set up and completed on the "Hollywood movie-making" model — talented people come together for a specific project, then move on to new projects

- But these free-agents don't just play ball for a living, they actually work. And they don't have agents to do marketing for them. Hence many of these free-agents can use help like this book.

Selling yourself as a consultant, free-agent, or specialist

Much—perhaps most—of the how-to information this book, *How to Sell Face-to-Face: Survival Guide*, will be equally useful if you happen to be "selling" yourself for a job opportunity as if you're selling your services as a free-agent, or if you're selling products.

That is, whether you're selling your invention (or software), your expertise (as a free-agent or consultant), or yourself (as a potential employee), most of the same approach and methodology applies. That consists of these tasks:

- You look for leads to the decision makers who can say yes;

- You approach them, which means finding a way through or around the "gates" they set up to guard their time;

- You make a strong—though brief and professional—impact on first contact with them;

- You research to find what needs you can fill, including asking smart questions during your initial meetings;

- You present your capabilities in ways that match those needs uncovered;

- You handle any questions and objections, not defensively, but rather by turning them around into points in your favor;

- You pick up subtle "buying signals" that clue you in on the other person's thinking;

- And, finally, you "close" each meeting with either a firm decision, or agreement on the next action step forward.

Selling face-to face

In this book, we'll be working together through the need-to-know steps of selling face-to-face, across the table from real prospects. That's why I call it *How to Sell Face-to-Face: Sales and Selling Survival Guide for People New to Sales and Selling*, with emphasis on the "survival guide" aspect, as well as the "new to sales and selling."

(Why do I repeat "sales and selling?" Ah, let's just say "for technical reasons" having to e-books and how they are marketed.)

Survival guides need to be as compact and "netted-out" as feasible, focusing on the "must-know now," leaving the theory and advanced stuff for later. It's designed to help you get selling face-to-face on Monday morning, not sitting home trying to pull out the need-to-know from a stack of other books.

The first step is the most important step

It's important at the start not to spend too much time reading and theorizing. Yes, do read here and get a sense of what to do and not do. But, before very long, try it. Jump in. Try making some sales calls.

After you've seen what sales calls are like, and gotten a feel for what potential prospects think of what you're offering—as well as what they ask about your product—then come back and spend some more time with this book, refining and rehearsing.

Michael McGaulley

There's an old saying about writing books that applies equally well to getting started selling:

First drafts are for getting it down on paper;

later drafts are for getting it good.

The lesson for you: accept the fact that your early sales calls may not be perfect. But you have to get past those "first drafts" so you can learn from them and make the later attempts better.

And there's another old saying with the same theme:

The perfect is the greatest enemy of the good-enough.

If you put off those first sales calls until you feel you have everything perfect, you may be so long that you miss the opportunity altogether. (I'm definitely not suggesting that you go out unprepared at the start: just prepare as much as you reasonably can, reasonably soon, then go try it in the real world . . . and learn.)

A helpful first step: ask potentials for advice and input

Maybe, even before you make your first "official" sales calls, you might want to make some calls for advice. Here's what I mean. Phone up a few people who fit the potential prospect "profile"— that is, people who might be users of what you are considering offering. When you phone them, make it clear you are asking their advice at this point, not trying to sell:

"I've developed a service in the area of _____, which I understand overlaps with your areas. Before I go too far down that road, I'm taking time to ask the advice of people knowledgeable in that field. Your name has been suggested as someone who is particularly knowledgeable.

Newbie's Guide to Selling Face-to-Face

"I'd very much appreciate the chance to come in for perhaps 15 minutes or so and tap your expertise. That is, I'd like your input on whether this is a viable product (or service), on how I might present it, potential users, and so on. I respect your expertise, and would very much appreciate your advice. Can you spare me some time?"

Key: if you say 15 minutes, *mean* it, and stick to that time limit . . . unless the other person clearly wants you to stay. Is 15 minutes enough time? Likely so, if you have your act together, and know what you're looking for. Should you ask for more than 15 minutes at the start? You can ask, but the more time you ask for, the less likely the other person will agree to meet.

You may feel, "I know what I'll be selling, and I know who needs it, so why waste time meeting these people at the start, even before I've locked in just what I'll be selling?"

- For one thing, these are easy meetings, and they give you a chance to feel what it's like to be sitting across the table from a potential prospect.

- The advice will usually be sound, because they're working in that field and that market. Their comments and suggestions may open up ideas and potentials that you may not have thought of on your own.

- Because you have asked for their advice and help, they may develop a sense of "ownership," and go out of their way to help you not only refine the idea, but as "owners" may make some phone calls to open doors to key prospective buyers.

- Best of all, they may buy. Probably not that day, but they may suggest that you come back when your product is ready to market.

Step 1: QUESTIONS FOR FOCUSING YOURSELF, YOUR BUSINESS CONCEPT, AND YOUR APPROACH

A key reality of sales life: even the best, most-experienced sales people *succeed only when they are selling what that prospect needs.*

That may surprise you. Like the rest of us, you've likely grown up with the old idea that a really good sales person can sell anything to anybody at any time, even, as the saying goes, Iceboxes to Eskimos.

But not so. No one can sell a Prospect anything which that Prospect does not need.

Okay, maybe that last statement is not exactly true. *Sometimes* sellers can lie, cheat, and bully a Prospect into buying something they don't need. But they will never get a second chance to make a sale, not with that purchaser, and not with anyone that purchaser warns off.

You can't sell what the Prospect does not need, but you can help that Prospect recognize that they have a need, that the need is important to fill, and that the solution you propose is the best way of filling that need.

That's what this little survival guidebook is all about: showing you how to help your prospects recognize—

- First, that they have a need for what you offer;
- Second, why it is important to make the investment required to fill that need;

- Third, that the solution you propose is the best way of filling that need—better than the present method (if any), and better than the solution offered by any of your competitors.

- (Incidentally, we'll generally be using the terms "product" and "service" interchangeably, so if you see one term, assume that what we say about it applies to the other, as well.)

Products or services?

Before you get into the process of selling, it's a good idea to gain fresh perspective on what you'll be offering by working through some key questions designed to help you look at your product or service from the perspective of the person across the table—the prospective buyer.

1. Who needs what I offer? How can I (and my product or service) help fill those needs?

Notice that the question is *not*, "What am I planning to sell?" because that's the wrong question.

The place to start is with potential Prospects' needs, and not with your product or service. What do they need, and how can I help fill that need?

But you may object, "Are you kidding? I've already got this wonderful product, and I'm not about to throw it away and start over." Or you may object, "I've built up a package of very valuable skills and expertise over my career, and there is no way I'm going to begin again as a novice!"

I'm not suggesting that.

Newbie's Guide to Selling Face-to-Face

What I am suggesting is that you step across the table and sit— mentally— in the Prospect's chair. Then ask, "If I were the Prospect, what would I be looking for — looking for, that is, in an area that I (the real me) can provide?"

Put differently, ask, "What can I do to help them? What do they need (whether or not they are presently aware of that need), and what is in my repertoire that can help fill that need?"

As you consider these questions, you'll likely make some very interesting and valuable discoveries, in areas such as —

• Who (or what organizations) have a need for what you can offer — and that list may be a lot wider than you had originally thought.

• Why they need what you offer — again, that list of needs may be different, and broader, than you were thinking.

• Ways in which what you were planning to offer can be modified, expanded, or simply expressed differently than you had assumed — hence opening a wider market, perhaps with stronger needs.

2. Why do they need it?

It's obvious— at least to you—all the wonderful things your product (or service) will accomplish.

But will all of that be so obvious to the Prospects you approach?

Perhaps not. Even if the uses are clear, the need for your product may not be so apparent.

Therefore, in preparing to sell, think backwards from your product or service to develop a clear perception of precisely how a

Prospect will be able to recognize a need for your product or service. Ask yourself questions such as,

- When my product is in place here, or my work has been completed, how will the client recognize that it has been successful?

- What needs will it have filled?

- For what kinds of situations would a satisfied customer recommend my product or service to someone else?

Once you have those needs in mind, use them as targets to work toward in structuring your selling strategy. If those indicators show that a need exists, then you want to find ways of helping that prospective buyer become vividly aware of these indicators and their significance.

Caution: Instead of asking about "needs," you could ask about the "problems" they face. But there's a strange difference in buyer psychology operating between the two words.

If you ask about problems, the sales Prospect will probably deny that any problems exist. After all, the existence of unsolved problems implies that they have been sub-par in some way in performing their duties as a manager or as a person. Good managers don't let problems continue.

But if you probe for what Needs exist, that's not so threatening, and you'll usually get a more open response helpful both to you and to the prospect you're there to assist.

3. What will my product (or service) DO for those who buy it? That is, what specific Needs will it fill? What service does it render? In short, how will it help them?

4. Why is it worthwhile to fill those needs? What direct costs and indirect consequences result from the unfilled needs?

5. Will my product not only fill the needs, but also help pay for itself in savings, or by opening other opportunities?

People (and organizations) don't buy THINGS; instead they buy the RESULTS flowing from those things or services.

For example, one doesn't buy a television set just to have a box with a screen on it, but rather to have a way of getting access to TV programs: those programs are the results flowing from investing in the television box.

When you look from the buyer's perspective, you'll see that the interest is not in the innovations and features of your product (or service), but rather how those features translate into practical ways that can make the things that matter to them operate better, more efficiently, more profitably, and so forth.

Putting that differently, if you are to sell effectively, there are two assumptions that you can not make:

First, you can't take for granted that the prospect is aware of a need for your product or service.

Probably the single most important part of your role as a sales person is to help the Prospect become aware of that need, or to become more aware of it. The stronger the Prospect's sense of need is, the greater will be your chances of making the sale.

Second, you can't take for granted that the prospect sees the link between his need and how your product or service can fill it.

Once the Prospect becomes aware of a need, the next part of your job is to help that Prospect see the link between the need and how your product or service can fill that need.

Those practical benefits are perfectly clear to you, but are almost certainly far less clear to the prospective customer who is seeing it for the first time.

Indeed, they may even be seeing a whole new concept or technology for the first time.

We'll be talking a great deal in this book about helping prospective customers develop an awareness of the needs which your product can fill. By thinking through in advance what those needs might be, you'll be better prepared to convince the customers to buy.

6. In 30 seconds or less, how will I sum up the essence of what kind of needs my product or service fills? Who does it help, and how does it help?

In sales jargon, this is the "Elevator Pitch." It's the short, smart, pithy, intriguing response you'd make if you're riding the elevator at a convention, or standing around before a Movers and Shakers Luncheon, and somebody asks what you do.

But short, smart, pithy, intriguing responses don't just happen: you need to invest time in advance thinking through and rehearsing so the words come out just right.

The key is to focus on what your product (or service) does for customers— that is, what needs it fills—rather than on what it is. Example: suppose you're asked that question of what you do.

Which of these responses do you find more powerful and compelling?

- "I design webpages to meet the new HIWE standard."
- "As a consultant, I help clients improve their internet marketing reach using new technologies just becoming available."

Answer: the second example, of course, because it focuses on what you do for your clients. The first example is too techie. The prospect may have no clue of the HIWE standard, and would very likely tune you out.

It may take time, and several early drafts, before you have the perfect Elevator Speech, so begin thinking about it early. But don't lock it into concrete too early. Be open to what the marketplace tells you as you are making your early sales calls.

You want to keep your options open so you can adapt to what opportunities open up, yet you do need to be able to speak of one or a few areas in which your experience is relevant as a way of setting the context of what you are capable of.

For example, you could say,

- "My experience has been in the general field of _____, and I'm adapting that expertise to problem-solving in related fields."

Or you could respond,

- "I'm basically a problem solver, working in the general area of ____."

If possible, immediately back up these general statements with a capsule summary of one or two relevant accomplishments:

"For a large manufacturing company, we _____. We anticipate offering those kinds of services to smaller firms in this area."

7. What, then, are my core selling messages?

If we could somehow replay all the sales calls that have been made since the beginning of time, I suspect we'd find that nearly as many prospects have been talked OUT of buying as have been talked INTO saying Yes. Why? Because the sales person either talked too much, or failed to provide concise, to-the-point, positive reasons for buying.

Therefore, as you refine your sales approach, work toward boiling down the essence of your selling messages into neat, succinct one or two sentence core messages.

That takes discipline. You know an enormous amount about your product and what it can do. In fact, you're probably bursting with all of the good reasons to buy. But often Less is More: to communicate, it's usually better to hit a few key points clearly than to overwhelm—and confuse—the prospective purchaser with a lot of not-necessarily-relevant detail.

8. Is there competition? If so, what is unique about my product/service?

Until you know who your main competitors are, along with what they charge, and their strengths, and weaknesses, you're not ready to sell.

Going further, until you can explain clearly and to-the-point why you are unique, you're not ready to sell. You can try to pretend the competitors don't exist, but they'll be on your prospects' minds.

Newbie's Guide to Selling Face-to-Face

In looking for what is unique about your product or service, keep in mind that your special advantages may come from factors such as,

- lower cost: this can take various forms, such as lower purchase price, or lower long-term operating costs, or lower personnel or training costs;
- better service;
- better financing terms;
- better timing— perhaps ability to get to work sooner, with no delays;
- your continuing personal involvement to ensure that it does all you claim it will.

Be sure to project yourself mentally into the mind of several different hypothetical customers. Look at your product, along with the service, purchase terms, and the like, with the same kind of hard-nosed realism that you would if you were actually the buyer instead of the seller. What questions would you be asking? What concerns would be in the back of your mind?

It's better to know them and prepare to deal with them now than when you are further down the line. If your product (or terms) have flaws, better to spot them yourself now than after you have committed more time and money.

Letting Your Competitors Educate You

There's another good reason for knowing who you competitors are: your competitors can be your best teachers:

- Your competitors can teach you by what they do or don't do, or are not doing well. You don't want to be a copy-cat, but if something works, you can learn from it, and tweak it into something better.

- Your competitors can teach you by the blunders they have made: there's no need to make your own mistakes if you can learn from those of others.

- Your competitors can point you to your specific niche in the market. By analyzing where your competitors are and are not, you can find where you can fit in and be unique, perhaps by a unique product, by cost, by overall cost savings, by quality of the service you provide, and so forth.

But what if there IS no competition?

That could, obviously, be very good news: you've got the market to yourself . . . at least for a while.

But the lack of competition could also be a warning signal. Better do some checking. It could be that someone has already tested the market, only to find it didn't pay off. Or perhaps what you're offering is too novel, and the market isn't—at least mentally—ready for it yet.

Newbie's Guide to Selling Face-to-Face

Summary: Starting questions

Before you get too far down the track, think through answers to eight key strategy questions:

1. In a nutshell, precisely what IS the product or service that I am offering?

2. Who needs my product or service?

3. What will my product (or service) DO for those who buy it? That is, what specific Needs will it fill? What service does it render? How will it help them?

4. Why is it worthwhile to fill those needs? What direct costs and indirect consequences result from the unfilled needs?

5. Will my product not only fill the needs, but also help pay for itself in savings, or by opening other opportunities?

6. What, then, are my core selling messages?

7. How can I most effectively bring my selling messages to prospects?

8. Is there competition? If so, what is unique about my product or service?

    - What can the competition teach me?

    - If there *is* no competition, what does that tell me?

Michael McGaulley

Step 2: DEVELOPING A LIST OF POTENTIAL PROSPECTS

Here's a checklist to trigger your thinking on other possible sources of leads:

1. **Best source of leads: Obvious or logical users of your product or service.**

You likely already know a lot of prospective users of your product or service. You may already know many of them by name. They may be people with whom you worked at your previous jobs. Or they may be your counterparts in other organizations, or people you know from professional or trade groups.

Others you may not know personally, but know who they are by the organization within which they work, and by their job title.

Or you may know that since they hold a particular kind of job, or live in a particular area, or have a particular kind of hobby, they are logical users of your product or service.

Gather names first, edit only later

Write these names down as they come to you, regardless of how remote the chances of selling them seem now. Develop your list of prospects first, and only later think about editing it down. The possibilities you list may trigger other ideas, referrals, and leads.

The worksheet below may help structure your thinking.

- List the prospects that occur to you in the left column.
- Then, in a word or two, sum up in the middle column why you think they are a good prospect.

- Finally, extend your thinking: given why this seems a good prospect, why do they seem promising, and who else might have similar needs?

Obvious/logical users	Why my product/service is good for them.	Who else (other potential prospects) may have similar needs?

2. Another source of leads: Your present contacts.

If you're marketing the expertise you gained in your former job, then the people you met while working there—both within that organization and in other firms—may be potentials.

Similarly, those you met through business and professional groups may be prospects for your services now, or may be able to suggest referrals for you to contact.

The people you know in a non-professional way may also be helpful contacts: people from your neighborhood, civic groups, church, circle of friends and acquaintances.

You may ask them for help when you see them face-to-face, or you may decide to phone them for ideas. You could contact them to get their ideas on potential prospects. Even better, you might ask for their suggestions on your whole business plan. They will be flattered that you asked for their input, and may well have some ideas that had not occurred to you.

3. **Getting leads from referrals.**

Ask for referrals from everyone who buys from you.

Also, ask for referrals also from those who don't buy . . . but do seem interested. Although they may not have the money or need right now, they may still think you have a worthwhile idea, and want to pass it on to friends.

To ask for a referral, simply say something to the effect, "By the way, is there anyone else you could suggest I contact?"

If they suggest a name, ask, "Do you mind if I mention your name when I call them?" If you're lucky, they may even offer to phone ahead and make the introduction for you.

If they have trouble coming up with names, gently prompt them by suggesting in a way like this: "Is there anyone else I should talk to in your company (or agency, if it is public sector)?"

Pause to give them time to think. Wait for an answer. If necessary, prompt again: "What about your counterpart in (other organizations)?"

4. **Gaining leads via prospects you attract.**

Additional leads may come to you from actions you take in venues, such as,

- Your appearances at trade shows and the like;
- Talks before groups of potential users, such as civic and professional organizations;
- Your blog, Facebook, Twitter, or other new media;
- Articles and interviews in trade journals and local media;

- Advertisements;
- Your contacts through civic organizations, volunteer work, and similar activities.

5. "Smokestacking" as a source of leads

The term comes from the days when sales-people new to a town would begin by driving around looking for the factory smoke-stacks, as the smoke-stacks usually indicated where the business in that town was. The smoke-stacks marked the factories, but also where some of the suppliers to the factories were located, as well as restaurants and the like.

Nowadays when smokestacking you would be looking for office buildings, industrial parks, shopping centers, and other clusters of activity that may contain the offices of likely prospects.

Generally, the most efficient way of smokestacking these days is to find your way to the Chamber of Commerce, which will supply you with maps, and directories of the businesses, non-profits, and governmental agencies in the area. Most of the time, you'll be able to determine from these lists which organizations are viable prospects, or at least worth further exploration.

Check also if there are regional development agencies in the area, as they would also have directories of manufacturers and other major industries. (The names of these kind of agencies will vary with your state or locale.) It may be helpful to call your state's Department of Commerce, or even the Governor's office, as these development or redevelopment agencies or authorities often either use public money, or are funded by state bonds.

But in some cases it will be helpful to go out and eyeball these business clusters, doing some on-site investigation. The directories may be a year or more old, and there may have been turnover. Or some organizations' names may be too vague to tell you what you need to know.

In some cases, you can generate leads by quick sweeps through office buildings and commercial clusters, hardly more than poking your head into each office to see if it would be worthwhile to schedule an appointment later.

6. Leads from your paper and internet research.

Here we get into a topic that's far too vast and too specialized for this book. However, before you bury yourself in your computer, don't forget the old-fashioned ways: telephone books, and local newspapers and magazines. And check out the business section in local libraries.

Summary/Action Plan

Before reading on, spend a few minutes making a first attempt at a concrete action plan to structure your search for prospects. Jot at least three ideas in each category.

1. Who are the obvious or logical users of your product or service?

2. Your existing contacts, perhaps from your previous work, from business and professional groups, or from civic, church, and other non-business groups.

3. Initial referrals. At the start, who might be able to help you generate lists of potential users, or make some introductions on your behalf?

4. Attracting prospects. Other than running ads, and giving talks, what other inexpensive, feasible ways are open to spread the word about yourself and your product?

5. Smokestacking. Are there office buildings, industrial parks, and the like where users of your product or service may tend to cluster?

6. Paper and internet research. Sure, the internet, but also what publications, directories, membership associations may help you locate potential buyers?

Step 3: FINDING YOUR WAY TO THE "PROSPECT"—THAT IS, THE PERSON OR TEAM WHO CAN SAY YES

1. You will make the sale *only if* you deal with the person or team who can say Yes to what you offer. That is the Prospect.

That's obvious enough, especially if you're selling to individuals.

But it may not be so easy if you're selling to organizations, because organizations are usually filled with people who can say no— but only no— to new ideas and new products.

That is, they have the authority to say No to you, but— regardless of what or how good a deal you offer— they are simply unable to say Yes. Saying yes is just not in their job-descriptions.

Which means, if you want to make the sale—and not just go through the motions—then you need to find your way to the person or team who can say Yes. (In this book, we'll be referring to that person or team as the "Prospect," with a capital P.)

An obstacle to overcome

Trouble is, before you can talk to that person who can say Yes, you often have to wend your way past other people who have only negative decision-making authority; they typically range from the guard at the plant gate, to the Purchasing Manager, to the CEO's secretary or assistant. These are Screens or Gatekeepers, and we'll be talking about them a little later.

2. The person who can say yes may not be easy to reach, but you will be wasting your time and opportunity if you try to make your case to anyone else.

People who can only say no are usually easy to reach. When you're new to selling, it's usually tempting to make your case to anyone who will listen to you in the hope that maybe, just maybe, something will come of it.

But that's usually not a good idea. The reality is that if the person can only say no, but not yes, then by making your case to them, you open yourself to the risk of losing the sale, even though you have no chance at all of making it. (And if they say no, then your sale is just as dead as if you had heard it from a person who could have said yes.)

A pair of cautions

First, people who can only say no may not admit it.

Second, people who can only say no may convey that no in a subtle, or even coded, way. For example, the secretary or junior executive to whom you give your sales presentation will typically not say no in a direct way. Instead, they may tell you that they will pass on the information to the boss.

That sounds encouraging. But it usually translates to no sale.

They may even have the best of intentions to carry your sales message upstairs. But then they may have second thoughts, and decide that they really don't want to take the risk of seeming to promote something that the boss probably wouldn't be interested in, anyway.

For them, at that point, it may seem that the safest thing is to forget they ever talked to you. After all, the reality is that their jobs don't depend on selling your product for you, so at best they're likely to give it one shot, and not push very hard.

If you call them to check on things, they'll tell you it's still pending, or else to fail to return your phone calls.

Even if they do follow through, and actually do carry your sales message to the boss, you can be sure that they aren't going to sell it as well as you could. After all, they don't know that much about your product, nor perhaps about the need it is designed to fill.

3. In finding your way to the person or team who can say yes, look for the presence of two factors: direct need, and budget dollars/buying authority.

If you're selling to individuals, or even to small organizations, you shouldn't have much difficulty in finding who the individual (or team) is who can say yes to what you offer. If you're selling to Joe's Roofing and Siding, talk to Joe.

It gets more complicated when you market to larger organizations, because the person who can say yes to one product, or in one price range, may not be able to say yes in other circumstances. The person who can buy $200,000 worth of computers may, ironically, not be the one to say yes to engaging your consulting services to develop software for those computers.

Nonetheless, the person who can say yes can usually be identified by **two key tests:**

First test: Who has a DIRECT NEED for your product/service?

General rule of thumb: Whenever possible, do not try to sell to the purchasing department . . . unless purchasing is likely to have a direct need for the product or service. (There are some exceptions, which we will talk about below.)

Instead, try to find your way around purchasing to the actual user of your product or service, so that you can make the case directly.

The advice to bypass purchasing may seem illogical: after all, you might think, Doesn't the Purchasing Department, by definition, do all of the organization's buying? Actually not.

In most cases, purchasing does not generate purchasing decisions, but rather coordinates the purchase of products and services for other departments.

What this means to you, in practical terms, is this: If you are selling a generic item, or a commodity, then purchasing may be the place to begin. This is especially true if you know that purchasing is already soliciting bids for what you offer. (But be warned: if you are selling something that is perceived as only a commodity, then generally the only way you can compete is on lowest price.)

But if you are selling something unique—such as your consulting services, or an innovative product—then you're much better off to find your way to the end user and make the case for yourself.

For similar reasons, it's usually best to bypass the Training and Personnel departments. In a way similar to Purchasing, Training and Personnel typically execute orders set by other departments.

If you're selling training programs, or if you're a consultant, you'll usually be far more successful if you get to the head of the department that will actually be using your services or products, and make the case directly there. That way, the manager can specify your training services by name, rather than taking a chance with an off-the-shelf product.

Second test: Does this person or team with direct need ALSO have budget dollars and buying authority?

If you're selling an item that is within the petty-cash limit, then almost anybody within the organization can buy it. But once you get above that limit, you need to learn more about the actual buying limits and procedures within that specific organization.

The central question to address is, Do the various levels of managers each have a fixed dollar amount up to which they can buy on their own authority, or are buying decisions made only at the top (or at least signed off there)?

If you're coming back to market to your previous employer, you may already know the answer. Similarly, if you have a contact within the Prospect firm, that person may be able to give you guidance.

We'll be looking for ways to check out budget, buying authority, and need in the remainder of this Step.

4. Be attuned to any significant "Decision Influencers."

A "Prospect," or "Decision Maker" (as we use the terms here), is a person (or team) with the Authority to buy, a Need for what you offer, and the budget Dollars required.

But don't overlook the importance of Decision Influencers. A Decision Influencer is a person or team who may not have direct need, and/or may not have budget dollars or buying authority, but may nonetheless may be the key factor in whether that organization buys what you are offering.

Implications: first, as you scout around, be alert to who these Decision Influencers may be.

Second, do not alienate them along the way: they may not have the title and power to say yes, but they may nonetheless have the ability to keep you from getting the sale.

Decision Influencers may include

- Those who will be the actual users of your product or service. For instance, in mid-sized companies and upward, the person who uses the computer you sell will generally not be the actual Decision Maker (because they are lacking one or more of the key elements of Authority to buy, Need for what you offer, and Dollars in the form of budget or spending authority). But, nonetheless, they will probably have a significant influence, as they are technically knowledgeable, and will be living with whichever computer is selected.)

- Financial advisors such as the firm's accountant or Chief Financial Officer may be Decision Influencers: they may say whether or not the firm can afford what you offer, and may also have input on finance alternatives, such as leasing versus purchasing, and the like.

- The Decision Maker's mentor may be a Decision Influencer. That is, the person who has Decision Making Authority, Need, and Dollars, may still want to check it with the old hand in the company who has helped him along the way. Chances are, you won't know who that Mentor is, and may never meet them; just be aware that there may be such a person, feeding suggestions, questions and other concerns to the Decision Maker.

- The Purchasing Manager may be a Decision Influencer. That influence may be more on the technical aspects of how to make the purchase happen within the organization's policies on purchasing. But because the Purchasing Manager may have this influence is a good reason not to antagonize him. Go around him to get to the real decision maker, but do it quietly and in a nice, unobtrusive way.

Summary: Finding your way to the Prospect— that is, the person or team who can say yes

1. You will make the sale only if you deal with the person or team who can say Yes to what you offer. That is the Prospect.

2. The person who can say yes may not be easy to reach, but it will be a waste of time and opportunity to make your case to anyone else.

3. In finding your way to the person or team who can say yes, look for the presence of two factors: direct need, and budget dollars/buying authority.

4. Work with any significant Decision Influencers.

Michael McGaulley

Step 4: INITIATING YOUR FIRST CONTACT

1. Cold-calling— that is, dropping by in the hope of meeting on the spot—is usually not a good way of making your approach.

True, if you cold-call, you're more flexible because you don't have to plan ahead: you don't need to invest time on the phone setting up appointments, or figuring out how much travel time to allow.

But cold-calling is usually not an efficient use of your time: you risk spending too much time hanging around waiting rooms, hoping for an opening to see the Prospect.

Even if you do get in to see the Prospect, they may be bothered by the interruption, or distracted by the thought of what they had been planning to do in this block of time. In short, you could end up spending entire days without making any real progress.

2. Rather than making cold-calls, it's generally much more efficient—and more professional—to invest the time in phoning ahead to set up appointments.

It's your call whether to set aside a block of time each day to call for appointments, or to phone in free time between other activities. But, bottom-line, the time you invest in calling ahead is always well-spent.

For one thing, you'll start each day with at least some solid appointments lined up. Because you have planned ahead, they will be geographically well-grouped in the same part of your working territory, and you won't waste time shuttling back and forth across the city.

Another advantage in phoning ahead: using techniques we'll examine shortly, you can use this initial phone conversation to subtly test whether this is in fact the right person to see—do they hold the job and responsibilities that you have been led to believe? Do they have at least some initial interest in what you are marketing?

Still another advantage of operating by appointment: you can go to the meeting better prepared. In most cases, the appointment will be scheduled for several days ahead. That gives you time to review your files on the organization, or to network with other contacts for insight on this organization and individual, and their likely hot-buttons.

Cold-calling: when it is appropriate

There are, however, a couple of instances in which it does make good business sense to drop in on an organization even without an appointment—that is, to cold call.

- Early on, such as when you drop by to do your initial research. That's usually a short call, and you can usually get most of the information you need without seeing the boss.

- Also, it is acceptable to drop by clients who are already using your product to check on how things are going. These also are usually short calls.

Summary: Initiating first your contact

1. Cold-calling – that is, dropping by in the hope of meeting on the spot – is usually not a good way of making your approach.

2. In most cases, instead of making cold-calls, it's much more efficient, and more professional, to invest the time in phoning ahead to set up appointments.

Michael McGaulley

Step 5: GETTING PAST THE GATE-KEEPER

1. When you phone the Prospect, be prepared to encounter a Gate-keeper, or Screen.

If you'll be selling to business people, bear in mind that they juggle a lot of calls on their time and attention. They're busy, and they want to focus on what they consider most important.

Chatting with unknown sales people is usually not high on their list of important things to do with their time. (Unfair? Maybe so, but it's your job to convince them why it is important to meet with you.)

In any case, many business people set up various kinds of gates or screens to minimize unimportant and unnecessary interruptions.

The Gate-keepers you are likely to encounter may begin with the security guard at the gate, include the receptionist, and extend to the administrative assistant who guards the final door to the Prospect's office.

An answering machine may also serve as a Gate-keeper: we'll focus on the how-to of answering machines and voice mail in item 3, below.

2. Bear in mind that this Gate-keeper is not there to keep you out; rather, their role is to protect the boss from unnecessary interruptions.

The Gate-keeper is in place to minimize distractions so the Boss can focus on what is truly significant to the organization.

What is truly significant? That depends on the context. A dentist may convey to the staff that what is truly significant is the time spent looking into patients' mouths. A shop-owner may be torn between spending time with customers, keeping up with paperwork, and ordering new merchandise.

The way to open the gate is to focus your introduction on whatever is truly significant to this unique Prospect. The Gate-keeper will open for you if, and only if, you communicate, through your words and professionalism (that is, your appropriate business telephone etiquette) that you have the potential of bringing something of significant value to the organization (your truly significant business purpose).

Business telephone etiquette

Business telephone etiquette with the Gate-keeper means,

- first, not coming across as rude or arrogant: they are only doing their job of shielding the person for whom they work;

- second, proper business telephone etiquette with the Gate-keeper focuses on helping them see why you and what you offer will be important to that executive—that is, by making it clear why this meeting is important to the boss;

- third, telephone etiquette in the business context means getting to the point, not wasting time in chit-chat, yet not appearing abrupt or condescending. (We'll get into this aspect below.)

How-to use "significant business purposes" as a key to open the gate

Though we use the term business purpose, the same concept applies if you are selling to non-profits, government organizations, or individuals: their significant purpose is what matters to them.

Tip #1. Make the Screen your ally.

When you phone, listen closely for the name of the person who answers, and then use that name: "Hello, Mr. Gordon, my name is _____."

People like to hear their name used. It's a token of respect, and makes the conversation more personal and human.

Another reason to listen closely to the name: this may be someone you met earlier when you were on the premises researching the organization as a potential client. If the name is familiar, remind them of your previous conversation so they can match a face with your voice on the phone.

Tip #2. If possible, mention the name of someone who referred you, or made some other kind of Pre-Introduction.

If you are calling this Prospect at the suggestion of another of your clients or of a mutual friend, make that clear at the very start, both to the Screen, and later to the Prospect: "I'm calling at the suggestion of Ralph Meador of Meador Associates."

If you already know the Decision Maker from another context, mention this to the Screen, but be careful how you word it. You don't want the Prospect to come to the phone—or to avoid you—because he thinks you're setting up a tournament at the country club, or asking for a donation to the college alumni fund.

Once you have set that other context as a door-opener, then quickly move on to your present business purpose.

Tip #3. Pre-sell the Screen. But speak only in broad concepts. DO NOT become drawn into the details.

In persuading the Screen to put you through to the Prospect, you'll obviously need to talk some about your business purpose for calling. But beware of saying too much.

Basic principle:

You cannot **make** the sale over the phone, but you **can lose** it.

When you're on the phone (particularly with the Gate-keeper), speak in overall conceptual terms of what your product or service WILL DO FOR the organization, not of what it IS, nor of its technical features.

The more you get into the details and specifics of what you are offering, the more reasons you'll give the Gate-keeper for keeping you out: "You say you work with computers? Well, there's no point in your seeing Mr. Chase, as we already have our own in-house computer expert."

Solution: in this case, do not say "computers." Instead, speak of "methods for increasing productivity," or "techniques for developing more efficient work-flows." That is, focus on concepts and end-results, not the how-to. Leave that for later.

Or say, "I'd like to speak to Mr. Dobson about some methods that may be able to increase your organization's productivity by ten-percent or more, as we have with other firms."

Tip #4.   If necessary, ask questions the Gate-keeper won't be able to answer.

The overall **p**oint to make is that you need to see the Prospect because you have a sound business purpose in mind—something that will help that executive or the organization work better.

But some Gate-keepers won't be satisfied with broad concepts—like efficiency, productivity, and the like.   As a ploy, they may

Newbie's Guide to Selling Face-to-Face

try to put you on the defensive by asking questions, trying to draw you into divulging the kind of details that they can use to say no. Remedy: if you encounter that, regain control of the situation by asking your own questions, as in this model dialogue:

Screen: What is it you want to talk to Mr. Builder about?

Sales person: Mr. Builder is the construction engineer on the PDM Center, isn't he?

Screen: Yes, of course. But why do you need to talk to him?

Sales person: I'm calling to determine whether the PDM Center is being built in accord with the NEPA Standards on hydro-thallaxic transfaxions. Can you help me with that?

Screen: I have no idea about that. For that, you'll have to talk to Mr. Builder. Hold, please.

With a little ingenuity you should be able come up with a repertoire of unanswerable questions like these. The questions should be relevant to the reason for your call to the Prospect, but more technical or detailed than a receptionist or secretary would be prepared or willing to address.

(P.S. I totally made up the jargonistic quasi-term, "hydro-thallaxic transfaxions," and –amazing!—you can find it on Google!)

Tip #5. As a last resort, call when the Screen is away.

If you find that, no matter what, you just can't get through the Screen, try phoning before or after normal business hours, or even over the lunch hour: Prospects—usually managers---tend to be at their desks earlier, or later, or both, to take advantage of the quiet time when the office is empty.

In off hours, Prospects often answer their own phones. If you do get the Prospect on the line, be particularly brief and to-the-point, respecting that she is in the office at this time precisely in order to avoid interruptions.

Especially when you are speaking to the Prospect, get to the point— FAST—both on the phone and later when face-to-face.

3. When voice-mail is the Screen.

Voice-mail forms another kind of gate, keeping you from talking directly to the Prospect in organizations both small and large.

Above all, don't try to wing your response. Decide just what message you want to leave, then boil it down so it gets quickly to the point. Rehearse your message until you can say it confidently and with a smile in your voice.

All set? Not quite. Before leaving your first message on a Prospect's voice-mail, call your own voice-mail and leave the same message. Analyze it, from a Prospect's perspective. Revise and rehearse it again until it is right.

Other considerations to settle before calling:

Should you leave a message on voice-mail, or keep trying to reach the Prospect directly?

If you leave your name, then you leave it in the Prospect's hands to respond. That means you lose control.

It gets awkward if the Prospect doesn't return your call: Does no response mean no interest, or just busy right now?

Newbie's Guide to Selling Face-to-Face

Here's a strategy that works for me: try calling a few times, not leaving your name. Call at different times, hoping to finally get the Prospect at the desk. If the pattern becomes clear that you're not likely to catch the person, then go ahead and leave your name and number. You may or may not get a call-back, but at least you have tried all paths.

Should the message you leave identify your company name, or your reason for calling?

If the Prospect thinks you are a potential buyer of his services, he will be more likely to return the call than if he knows you are doing the selling.

On the other hand, a busy Prospect may not bother returning voice-mail calls that lack information. The best approach is usually to speak clearly, saying your name, maybe your company name (if you operate under a company format), and your phone number.

Tip: ever find yourself frustrated by people who leave you voice-mail, but then do a fast-mumble of their phone number, so you have to listen to the whole message again? They've said that number so often that easy to take for granted that everyone knows it. Do you really want Prospects to have to replay, and replay again, to pick up your call-back number?

Definitely do not try to make the sale, or even describe your product, over voice-mail.

Reason: You can only lose the sale via voice-mail, but you cannot make the sale.

Summary: Getting past the Gate

1.   When you phone the Prospect, you may encounter a Gate-keeper, or Screen.

2.   Bear in mind that Gate-keeper is not there to keep you out; rather, their role is to protect the boss from unnecessary interruptions.

Tip #1. Make the Screen your ally.

Tip #2. If possible, mention the name of the person who referred you, or perhaps made some other kind of Pre-Introduction.

Tip #3. Pre-sell the Screen, if possible. But speak only in broad concepts. DO NOT become drawn into the details.

Tip #4.   If necessary, ask questions the Screen won't be able to answer.

Tip #5.   If nothing else works, call when the Screen is away.

3.   On those occasions when voice-mail is the Screen, settle these issues in your mind before you place the call:

- Will you leave a message on voice-mail, or keep trying to reach the Prospect directly?

- Whether the message you leave should identify your company or your reason for calling?

- What will you say to intrigue the Prospect without saying so much that he or she can cross you off?

Step 6: MAKING YOUR FIRST PHONE CONTACT WITH THE PROSPECT

Seconds count once you get past the Screen and have the Prospect on the line. In most cases, the first 30 seconds on the line make or break the call. This is not the time to be fumbling for words, or wasting that precious time on "ice-breakers".

Think of this initial call for an appointment as the "Call-up, fix-up, hang-up." That is, *Get* the person on the phone, get to the point, then *get* off the phone.

The Prospects you phone during the business day are going to be involved in other work as you call, and usually will not have the desire or the time to get tied up in an extended phone conversation.

Besides, every minute that you're on the line raises the odds of another interruption coming in, so get to the point and complete your objective before you're bumped.

> 1. **This first phone contact is *not* the place to try to make your case. You can only *lose* the sale, but *not make it*, over the phone.**

Notice that this "Call-up, fix-up, hang-up" phase of the selling cycle does not include "Sign-up," because, no matter how much you say, or how great the discounts you offer, you cannot make the sale over the phone.

But—a big but—you can talk yourself out of the chance of meeting face-to face, and hence out of making the sale altogether. When it comes to the telephone, the less said the better.

This caution against making the case over the phone does not apply if your full selling cycle occurs over the phone. Telephone marketing (or "telemarketing") is useful with certain products (usually relatively low-cost items that don't require face-to-face contact. Telemarketing is not a subject we address in this book.

2. Once you have the Prospect on the phone, aim to accomplish three key tasks within the first 30 seconds.

This is a business call, not a social call, so in most cases it's best to get right to business. You are most likely to have the Prospect's full attention during the first half-minute of the call, so use those 30 seconds productively by getting on with these three essential tasks:

- Introduce yourself and your company.

- Excite the Prospect's interest in meeting with you to find out more.

- Ask the Prospect to meet at a specific time.

"Excite" and "interest" are both key words. In your short phone statement, focus on what you can do for the Prospect, not the details of what your product or service is.

The object at this point is to whet the Prospect's interest, not to satisfy it. After all, if you satisfy the Prospect's interest over the phone, then there is no need for her to meet face-to-face.

Accomplishing these three tasks of introducing yourself, exciting interest, and asking for a meeting may seem like a lot to accomplish in 30 seconds, but it can be done, as in this example:

"Mr. Whidby, this is Tina Rowland, of the Rowland Consulting Group. I'm calling because I'd like the opportunity to show you how we have boosted the profitability of firms like yours by as much as ten percent over a six-month period. The meeting would take about 20 minutes. I'm going to be in Hopkinsville next week on Tuesday morning and Friday afternoon. Which would be better for you?"

> **3. Make it clear at the start of the call if you are following up at the request of this Prospect, or if you are acquainted from another context.**

Example:

"You may recall that we met last month at the GTS Trade Show, where we discussed the effect of _____. I've given some thought to what we discussed then, and I have some ideas that might be of help to you. I could stop by to share these ideas with you sometime—perhaps on Monday afternoon? Or would later in the week be better for you?"

> **4. One of the best tools for exciting the Prospect's interest in meeting with you is a referral from someone they know and respect, or who has similar job responsibilities in another firm).**

Earlier, we addressed the benefits of using referrals as a way of breaking through the screen. Referrals are equally useful when speaking to the Prospect herself:

"As I mentioned to your secretary, I'm calling at the suggestion of Robert Clarkson at GNI Software."

Another example, this time tying the request to meet into the initial statement:

"I'm calling at the suggestion of Doreen Masters, who I believe you know through the local Step of the Computer Design Professionals' Association. She knows of my work, and thought it would be of particular interest to you."

You may need to pause a moment for the name to register, then go on to say,

"I'm going to be in Hopkinsville next week on Tuesday morning and again on Friday afternoon, and am free to meet either time. Which would be better for you?"

It's even better if the person who referred you is already a customer:

"I'm calling at the suggestion of Robert Clarkson at GNI Software, who's been a client of ours for about a year now. Perhaps he has mentioned our work to you?"

If your referral has called ahead to introduce you, so much the better. If not, move on to the core of your message:

"As we've been able to help GNI, I believe we may also be able to help you, and I think it would be beneficial for us to meet to explore your situation. Would you be free, say, tomorrow afternoon, or would Friday morning be better for you?"

Unless you're certain that the present Prospect and your referral face exactly the same need, it's best to leave open just how you can help. If you get drawn into the details of what you did for this other client, there's a risk that your new Prospect may respond with words to the effect, "Well, that sounds nice, but we don't need anything like that."

The point of the reference is to establish your credibility, not to suggest that the other project would be an exact template for this situation.

Newbie's Guide to Selling Face-to-Face

Summary: Your first phone contact with the Prospect

1. Think of this initial call for an appointment as the "Call-up, fix-up, hang-up." That is, Get them on the phone, get to the point, then get off the phone.

2. his first phone contact is not the place to try to make your case. You can only lose the sale, but not make it, over the phone.

3. Once you have the Prospect on the phone, aim to accomplish three key tasks within the first 30 seconds.

4. Make it clear at the start of the call if you are following up at the request of this Prospect, or if you are acquainted from another context.

5. One of the best tools for exciting the Prospect's interest in meeting with you is a referral from someone they know and respect (or who has similar job responsibilities in another firm).

Michael McGaulley

Step 7: PREPARING FOR YOUR FIRST FACE-TO-FACE WITH THE PROSPECT

1. Always call ahead to confirm that the meeting is still on schedule.

Don't leave home without (well, without your American Express card, to be sure) but also without taking the time to call ahead to confirm that the meeting is still on schedule.

You might be reluctant to make that call to confirm, fearing that opens up the chance for a cancellation. There is always a risk of that, sure.

But the greater risk is to invest your finite time in traveling across town to that meeting only to find it has been postponed—perhaps for a few minutes, or even to another day.

Calling to confirm will prevent many wasted trips.

Besides, it conveys that you respect the value of your own time . . . which in turn subtly communicates that you are a serious professional.

Important: When you call to confirm, have your appointment book open and ready so you can quickly suggest alternate times if necessary.

When to confirm

When to make that call to confirm? Do it either earlier on the day of the scheduled meeting, or late afternoon of the day before for an early morning appointment.

If possible, confirm through the secretary or Gate-keeper, instead of disturbing the Prospect herself. Make it clear that you are making this call to confirm an existing appointment, and that you are already on the Prospect's calendar:

"Good morning. This is Paula Krantz with Adaptron Consultants. I'm calling to confirm my three o'clock meeting with Mr. Benson. Is that still on schedule?"

If there is a change of time or location, always echo that change, to confirm that you are both in accord:

"Agreed: we're shifting things back an hour, so now I'll be meeting with Mr. Benson at three-thirty this afternoon."

If you find you have to "re-sell"

When you call to confirm, there is always the chance that the Prospect may have decided that she now doesn't want to meet, after all. Therefore, when you call to confirm, be prepared to "re-sell" yourself.

Re-selling the idea of meeting is easiest if the Prospect herself comes on the line to tell you.

Deal with it as an objection: probe the reason, and then respond accordingly. (We examine how to deal with objections in Step 15.)

But what if the Prospect leaves it to the secretary to tell you that the meeting is postponed, or even canceled?

Start with the assumption that this hitch is just a scheduling matter, and suggest alternate times for rescheduling.

If that doesn't work, then try to find the real reason for the cancellation: it could just be their busy time of the year or month.

If the secretary says the Prospect doesn't want to meet at all, probe further to find why.

In any case, whether you talk with the Prospect, or with a Gatekeeper, try to avoid letting the door close permanently. Say something like, "Well, I would like to keep in touch, and perhaps we can talk again in a few months." Most will agree (if for no other reason than to end the conversation).

Thus when you make that call-back in a few months, you can then say that you had mutually agreed to talk at this time.

2. When you arrive on-premises . . .

Here we're focusing on a call on a business person in an office, but the principles apply whatever the place and Prospect.

As you walk into the office, try to carry your briefcase in your left hand, leaving your right hand free for retrieving business cards and hand-shaking. That avoids the awkward moments of setting things down to shift hands.

For the same reason, keep a supply of your business cards in the right pocket of your jacket. If you don't have a pocket, hold the card ready in your right hand before you enter the office so you won't be fumbling for it when you're standing in front of the receptionist or Prospect.

As you give the receptionist (and maybe later the secretary) your business card, introduce yourself and make it clear that you are expected by the Prospect at a specific time, (as otherwise you could be shuffled onto the drop-in list). Here's a model to adapt:

"I'm Paula Krantz, Adaptron Consultants, here for my four o'clock meeting with Mr. Benson."

Important: Do not hand over any sales literature at this point. It's essential that you control the information flow in the meeting. If you hand out literature too soon, chances are you'll find the Prospect flipping through your materials, instead of giving full attention to what you have to say.

3. Use the waiting time in the reception area to do your personal "industrial espionage".

You can often pick up a great deal of useful information in the few minutes before your meeting. (Count that as another very good reason for arriving early.)

Visual indicators

Use the waiting time to look around the place (including the building as you arrive).

- What do the location, furnishings and equipment tell you? That the organization goes for the best, regardless of cost? Or that economy and practicality reign here? Do the furnishings show that the emphasis there is on showing money, saving money, or making money? (For that insight, thanks to my wife, Susan, drawn from her experience as an executive search consultant.)

- (Indicators like these guide you in deciding whether to emphasize, for example, the high-tech, newest-of-the-new nature of your product, or instead to focus on how it is relatively low-cost, yet at the same time a cost-saver.)

- What is the "mood" of the place? Tense, stressed, to-the-point? (If so, maybe your product has the potential of reducing that work overload.)

Newbie's Guide to Selling Face-to-Face

Develop your own checklist of the kinds of specific clues that may indicate a need for your product or service.

Picking up clues from the literature in the waiting room

The scrapbooks, piles of magazines, and even the photos on the wall in the reception area may also provide useful clues on trends to address in your sales call.

- First priority: look at any publications put out by this Prospect organization, such as the annual report, newsletters, book of news clipping, and the like. From them you may get a sense of the priorities, as well as the insider jargon that operates there now. (Thus, if they are talking cost-cutting, you will want to talk cost-cutting. If they speak of the need to increase productivity, then speak of how your product/service can help do that.)

- Look also at any of this firm's brochures, catalogs, and other sales literature, as you may find other clues on need-areas you can fill. (As non-profits often rely on grants and government contributions, be attuned to any current relevant trends and buzz-words.)

- If this is a non-profit group or government agency, scan the literature for trends, as well as for projects under development, opening of satellite offices, and the like.

- Magazines and newsletters specific to the industry or profession in which that Prospect operates will give you a sense for what trends are important now. You may be able to relate these trends and other information to the benefits of your product or service. (The trade magazines may also give you names of other firms that may be potential customers.)

Michael McGaulley

Summary: Preparing for your first face-to-face with the Prospect

1. Always call to confirm that the meeting is still on schedule.

2. When you arrive on-premises . . .

3. Use waiting time in the reception area to do your personal "industrial espionage."

Step 8: OPENING YOUR FIRST FACE-TO-FACE WITH THIS PROSPECT

1. Enter the Prospect's office consciously projecting confidence.

Face it: if you're like most of us, you're probably not going to feel particularly confident as you set out on those first sales calls, But you can't let that show. Like it or not, there is an element of drama—even of acting—in sales. Your goal is to project energy and confidence in yourself and the quality of what you are selling.

You may think, "I'm a technology nerd (or a consulting economist, or whatever), and people are going to buy from me because of my wizardry, not because of my charm, personality, or dramatic flair."

True and false. They may ultimately buy on account of your wizardry (or easy payment terms, and so forth). But if you make a poor initial appearance, particularly if you project a serious lack of confidence in yourself or your product, they may tune you out long before you get to make your case.

2. Introduce yourself, offer another business card, and be prepared to shake hands.

Enter with your briefcase in your left hand in order to leave your right hand free, so you will be prepared to shake hands, if appropriate.

You have already given one business card to the secretary, but cards are good advertising, and don't cost much. Therefore, unless you actually see the secretary pass the card, reach into your right jacket pocket and get another card ready to pass on to the Prospect.

It's important to have that card in front of the Prospect now, while you're there, so she's not distracted by trying to recall your name.

You also want it handy so that the Prospect is prompted to stick it into her card index as you leave. (The Prospect will generally give you a card in return. Establish a system so that incoming cards automatically go in a different pocket than the one you use hold your own cards. That way, you won't risk giving one Prospect's card to another.)

Do not give the Prospect any sales literature yet; otherwise she will probably spend much of the time looking through it, instead of listening to you with full attention.

Note the wording above: "be prepared to shake hands."

Nowadays, a lot of people are not comfortable shaking hands — especially during flu season!—

so be sensitive to the Prospect's cues.

3. Open the call by reviewing the hot-button that got you this appointment.

What if the Prospect has forgotten who you are, or why she agreed to meet with you?

That's not unusual, and it doesn't mean that the sale is already lost. More likely, it's just that a lot has happened in the days since you called for the appointment.

Regardless of whether or not the Prospect recalls you, begin by briefly reviewing the "hot button" that in your earlier phone conversation persuaded her to agree to this meeting.

"As I mentioned in our phone conversation last week . . ."

4. If possible, follow up with a brief success story or mini-case study.

Both your opening refresher of what caught interest on the phone, as well a follow-up success story must be truly brief, as you don't want to get bogged down at this point. Here's an example of using the refresher of the earlier hot-button together with a follow-on mini-success story:

First refresher:

"As I mentioned on the phone last week, we're a consulting firm specializing in helping small firms like yours increase profitability by installing systems to speed up the billing process."

Immediate follow-on mini-case study:

"For example, at a small law firm in Greenville, we reduced the billing and collection cycle by an average of nine days per account, which translated into savings of around $500 per month. I'm here because I think we may be able to help your firm in a similar way. I'd like to begin by asking a few questions so I can get a sense of precisely how and where we can best focus."

(We'll be examining ways of using questions as selling tools in Step 10.)

Another example:

Refresher:

"As I mentioned in our phone conversation the other day, I called at the suggestion of Janet Squiers, who I believe is your counterpart at Amalgamated Industries. Perhaps she called you directly? I know she was enthusiastic about the service I offer, and suggested that perhaps it would be as helpful to you as it has been to her group."

Then the immediate follow-on mini-case:

"I don't want into too much detail about our work with Ms. Squiers' group, but I do feel free to say that we were able to reduce production overtime by about three-percent, resulting in cost savings of at least $1,000 per month."

Still another example:

Refresher:

"As I mentioned when we talked the other day, I'm here to introduce you to some of the methods my firm has used to boost the profitability of organizations like yours, by as much as ten-percent."

Mini-case:

"I realize that a ten-percent profits boost may seem almost too good to be true, given today's tough business conditions, but we did just that with QRS Industries in Riverwood. Today I'm here to explore the possibilities with you. With your permission, I'd like to ask a few preliminary questions to get a sense of your operation and where the possibilities may exist."

Caution: In this opening statement, the 30-Second Rule applies. What's the 30-Second Rule? Simply this: If you talk more than 30 seconds at a time, then you're almost certainly talking too much.

This is especially true early in the call, when you are just getting acquainted with the Prospect.

Don't talk on and on. Leave openings for the Prospect to respond and react; first, so that she doesn't begin to tune out the sound of your voice; second, so she has a chance to give you feedback (which you can then use to shape your approach).

5. Recommendation: Use "hot-buttons," *not* "ice-breakers" to open the call.

"Good morning, Mr. James. It's nice to meet you," is a normal courtesy as you enter the Prospect's office.

But suppose you then say, "Is that a golf trophy I see over there on your book-case? I take it you're quite a golfer." That is an ice-breaker.

In most situations, using an ice-breaker is a very bad way to open the call.

First, you're there on business, not for on a social call, so get down to business.

Second, ice-breakers risk being perceived as attempts to ingratiate and manipulate, as in the golfing example above.

Third, if you're so easily distracted by a golf trophy, the Prospect may think you're not very serious about your work.

Bottom-line, the reality is that ice-breakers are most often used as a crutch by sales people who are afraid to launch into the heart of the call. The Prospect may sense this, and peg you as weak.

*Exception: when an ice-breaker **may** be appropriate*

However, in some areas, typically smaller towns, ice-breakers are customary . . . so much so that if you do not open with some pleasantries, then you may be perceived as "a hard-driving city-slicker."

Another case in favor of using an ice-breaker arises if you already know the Prospect from another context. It would seem odd if you ignored the fact that you rubbed shoulders the previous week on the golf course, or at a Rotary luncheon.

When you do use ice-breakers, be attuned to the Prospect's signals that it's time to move on to business. A change in expression or posture, or a brief shift in eye contact often indicate that it's time to move on.

Before using an ice-breaker, ask yourself: Is my real reason for using this ice-breaker to allow us to get in accord, or am I using it as a procrastination tool to avoid getting down to business?

6. Be prepared for the possibility that the Prospect may start by saying she has had second thoughts and thinks it isn't a good idea to meet, after all.

Hearing that can come as a shock. You might be tempted to say, "Then why the #%&## didn't you say that earlier, before I spent an hour driving here?" Satisfying as that may be, it would probably not get you the sale. There are more productive approaches:

First, briefly review the hot-button that led the Prospect to agree to this meeting when you set up the appointment on the telephone. That refresher may be all you need.

Be ready to follow that with one or more additional brief reasons that indicate that it will be worthwhile to meet. Also, mini-case studies of your successes with other local firms are ideal here. (See the example earlier in this Step.)

"I certainly understand, Mr. Harkness, how busy it can get some days. But I'd just like to remind you that when we talked last week, I raised the possibility that the D-SPAN system would be a key factor in increasing productivity here.

Newbie's Guide to Selling Face-to-Face

"For example, Sylvia Atkins at Hamilton Packaging installed the D-SPAN a year ago, and mentioned last week that her accountant has been able to document direct savings of over $4,500 since then.

"You seemed intrigued by the Prospect of what D-SPAN can do when we talked on the phone; I think it will make even more sense if we can take a few minutes to examine the possibilities. I could do that now, being as brief as possible to respect the time crunch you're under, or I could return early next week. Which would be better for you?"

If that doesn't reawaken the Prospect's interest, treat this new reluctance to meet as you would an objection. We'll be examining objections and how to respond to them in Step 15.

Summary: Opening your first face-to-face with this Prospect

1. Enter the Prospect's office consciously projecting your confidence.

2. Introduce yourself, offer another business card, and be prepared to shake hands.

3. Open the call by reviewing the hot-button that got you this appointment.

4. If possible, follow with a brief success story or mini-case study.

5. In most situations, use "hot-buttons," not "ice-breakers" to open the call.

6. Be prepared for the possibility that the Prospect claims to have had second thoughts, and thinks it isn't a good idea to meet, after all.

Step 9: WORKING WITH THE PROSPECT TO UNCOVER NEEDS FOR WHAT YOU OFFER

1. People and organizations rarely buy products or services. Rather, what they DO buy are way of filling needs which they consider important.

2. A FEW products can create their own sense of need. But it's dangerous to rely on this as your main selling strategy.

It's risky to begin your sales call by focusing on your product. That's the "Dump it on the desk and hope they like it" selling strategy.

It might work, you might get lucky: it could happen that you're offering precisely what the Prospect has been looking for. Or it could be that the Prospect likes the look of it, or for whatever reason feels it's a "must-have."

The "Dump it on the desk" strategy works best when you're operating out of a shop or display area where the customers come to you. The very fact that they have come to you indicates that they have at least some sense of a need (or a want) for what you offer.

But, even then, it's risky to rely completely on the product to build the Prospect's sense of need. If it doesn't immediately "click" with them— that is, if they don't like it at first glance—then you are likely to find yourself stranded, with no real way to capture the sale from that point.

Sure, you can try to salvage the sale by going back to point out potential needs, but that's usually an uphill struggle this late in the process: It appears that you are scrambling to stay in the game. It's a lot more credible—and efficient—to begin by creating (or enhancing) the sense of need, and only then going on to show how your product can fill that need.

3. **The more strongly the Prospect "feels" a sense of need, the greater are your chances of making the sale.**

4. **The best way of creating or enhancing the Prospect's sense of need for what you offer is to ask the kind of questions that lead the Prospect to tell you why she needs it, and why it will help pay for itself.**

You might think that the most efficient approach is the direct approach: that is, simply to tell the Prospect why he needs your product. But that raises the issue of credibility: Would that Prospect really believe your telling him that he needs what you're selling?

Think of it the other way round: When you are a potential buyer, don't you find yourself discounting much of what the sales person tells you—writing off most of it as sales "puffery?" You listen, you may accept some of it, but you are not likely to believe it, at least not 100%.

How to deal with this? How can you induce the Prospect to believe that there is a significant need for what you offer?

Suppose this Prospect heard himself telling you not only why he needs the product, but even how it can help pay for itself?

The Prospect might be hesitant to believe a sales person, but how could he not believe what he's just heard himself saying?

But . . . short of hypnosis (or magic), how do you get a Prospect to tell you why she needs your product, and to tell you why it makes "dollars and cents sense" to fill that need?

How? By asking the right questions, listening closely to the response, then perhaps asking another follow-up question or two.

> **5. One reason for asking these questions is to help you understand the Prospect's situation, and to explore what needs exist.**
>
> **6. A second reason for asking the questions: in order to "take the Prospect with you" as you explore, so that both you and the Prospect gain a shared awareness of each step in the process.**

Therefore, even if you are totally confident that you already know that the customer needs your product, it still is essential to take him step-by-step with your through your analysis. Taking the Prospect with you through your analysis ensures that he becomes aware of the same evidence that you do, and hence comes to the same conclusions.

Bear in mind that the Prospect at this time is undertaking a couple of big mental leaps.

The first leap is to recognize and acknowledge that a need exists. (Previously, he may have accepted the status quo as a given, imperfect as it may have been. "We've always had problems with _____. That's just the way things are here.")

The second leap the Prospect makes is to see the link between that need and the capability of your product or service to fill the need.

These are major mental leaps, so it's important to take the Prospect with you, step by step, as you analyze the situation and recommend a solution. You can't afford to take for granted that what is obvious to you is equally obvious to the Prospect.

7. Therefore, ask the questions even if you are sure you already know the answers.

The needs of this Prospect might be different from the needs of all of the other Prospects you've encountered.

For that matter, what you hear from this Prospect may open your eyes to some additional latent potential within your product.

For instance, if you're selling to law firms, you might assume that after you have talked to a hundred similar firms, you know what the needs of firm #101 will be. Maybe so.

But, then again, maybe not. And what you learn about the special needs in firm #101 may open up a whole new area of potential, giving you a solid reason to go back and revisit all of those you've met with before, though this time now proposing a practical new use for your product.

Summary: Working with the Prospect to uncover needs for what you offer

1. People and organizations rarely buy products (or services). Rather, what they DO buy are way of filling needs that they consider important.

2. A FEW products can create their own sense of need. But it's dangerous to rely on that as your main selling strategy.

3. The more strongly the Prospect "feels" a sense of need, the greater are your chances of making the sale (provided, of course, that your product offers a good way of filling that need).

4. The best way of creating or enhancing the Prospect's sense of need for what you offer is to ask the kind of question that lead the Prospect to tell you why she needs it, and why it will help pay for itself.

5. One reason for asking these questions is to help you understand the Prospect's situation, and to explore what needs exist.

6. A second reason for asking the questions: to take the Prospect "with you" as you explore, so you both have a shared awareness of each step in the process.

7. Therefore, ask the questions even if you are sure you already know the answers.

In short, as you work with the Prospect, view your role as that of a consultant there to analyze and solve problems, not just to "push" one particular solution. We'll get into the how-to of that in the following Step.

Step 10: CONSULTATIVE SELLING: SELL BY ASKING SMART QUESTIONS

As we discussed in Step 9 . . .

One reason for asking these questions is to help YOU understand the Prospect's situation, and to explore what needs may exist for what you offer.

A second reason is to make sure the Prospect "tracks with you" through each step as you point out needs, and point out as well the value of filling those needs.

Therefore, ask the questions even if you are absolutely certain that you already know the answers.

1. **In your work with the Prospect, view your role as that of a consultant working to analyze and solve problems, not just to "push" one particular solution.**

Of course you want to sell your product — after all, that's what you're in business for. The Prospect knows that . . . and respects it; that's a given. However, by remaining objective, you build credibility with the Prospect, which is vital to a long-term relationship.

The kind of approach I suggest you take in working with the Prospect is very similar to the analytical method you would use if you were a management consultant working with the client.

"Consultative selling" is, very basically, helping Prospects solve problems. The focus is not on the product or service offered, but rather on defining the Prospect's needs, and the value of filling them.

2. **Important: before asking any questions, begin by setting the context for those questions: that is, briefly explain why you are asking.**

3. **Your opening question will usually involve asking the Prospect to give you a brief overview of the relevant area. Your specific questions will flow from the potential areas of need suggested by that overview (combined with your knowledge of what to look for).**

Some Prospects may be surprised to encounter sales people who begin by asking questions rather than by dumping their product on the desk and telling how wonderful it is. They may not be accustomed to this approach, and may wonder why you're asking, not telling.

Thus it's good to explain your reason for asking these questions right at the start. Example:

"As I mentioned on the phone, I'm here because I believe that my firm can help yours operate more profitably. Before we can be sure just how we can help, I'd need to know a little more about your firm (or department, etc.). Perhaps you would give me a brief overview of how many people you have in this department, and a general sense of the work flow--just an overview."

Another example:

"We've been able to help a number of other firms like yours, but so I can better target my ideas, I'd appreciate your taking a couple of minutes to give me a brief overview of the kinds of activities carried on in this section."

4. In asking your questions, it's usually best to work from broad to specific. That is, first developing context, then focusing in on areas of potential need, and only then on the value of filling those needs.

First, exploring from broad overview to a more narrow, specific focus helps you get a better understanding of the situation, and hence of the Prospect's real needs.

Second, the question-and-answer process takes the Prospect with you step-by-step, working with you through the reasoning process. In responding to your questions, the Prospect puts into her own words the situation as it exists, including the need for your product.

Finally, by working through a careful, objective approach to the situation, you enhance your credibility by demonstrating that you are a solver of problems, not just a "pusher of product."

5. OVERVIEW: begin with Overview questions asking the Prospect to give you broad perspective on the situation and context.

The Overview questions you ask should be broad enough to provide you an general sense of the situation. In a nutshell, the model Overview question is,

"So that I can better understand the situation, would you give me a brief overview of (your operation, office, etc.)?"

> Jot at least one **Overview question** appropriate to the calls you will be making.

6. **FOCUS-IN: once some possible need areas open up, ask Focusing-in questions that build from what has turned up and invite the Prospect to provide more detail on the specific needs that may exist.**

Focusing-in questions explore areas that suggest there may be a need for your product or service. The aim of the questions is to get the Prospect to say, in his or her own words, what those needs are, as well as why it is important to fill them.

The model Focusing-in question is,

"You mentioned that there seem to be some difficulties in _____. Could you tell me more about that? What effect does it have?"

> Jot at least one **Focusing-in question** appropriate to the calls you will be making.

7. **VALUE: Finally, ask Value questions to lead the Prospect to provide specific information—usually in terms of dollars—that establish both–**

   – what the need is costing (directly or indirectly), and,

   – the value of filling that need.

Value questions ask the Prospect to estimate what those unfilled needs are costing both directly and indirectly. You can then take the figures from those estimates and use them to show how your product can at least partly pay for itself, perhaps by filling that need or needs.

Model Value questions:

"When that difficulty occurs, what effects result? Does it, for example, cost you wasted time or money? Does it ever cost you good-will with your customers? How often? Can you put an estimated dollar value on these results when they occur?"

> Jot at least one **Value question** appropriate to the calls you will be making.

For a checklist with examples of each of these three types of questions, see the Supplement at the end of this Step.

8. As the Prospect provides the overview, listen for the indicators that suggest there may be potential need. Focus-in on these for more detail.

9. Since you are already an expert in what your product (or service) can do, you begin with a good idea of what kinds of indicators you are looking for, and hence where your questions should lead.

You know what your product is, and you have a good sense of what kinds of needs it can fill. Experience has shown you what types of indicators typically evidence a need for your product (and you will have been listening for these factors as the Prospect provides the overview you asked for).

For example, suppose you are marketing your consulting services, and your specialty is improving productivity within offices. Your ear is attuned to what kinds of practical indicators suggest that there is a need for your expertise. These indicators might include words like "bottlenecks," "delays," "late shipments," and "excessive overtime."

As you listen to the Prospect's overview, be particularly alert for indicators like these, whether expressed directly in those terms, or through examples that point in that direction. (But do not interrupt the Prospect yet. Let the overview run, as additional need-areas may emerge.)

When the overview concludes, pick up on what seems to be the most promising of these need areas, and ask focusing-in questions in order to explore this potential.

Your objective here, bear in mind, is to get the Prospect to tell you, in her own words, what that need is, and what practical implications flow from it. (Listen well to these answers, as you will later be quoting those words back to the Prospect as reason for buying your product.)

For example, in marketing your services as an office productivity consultant, you might ask focusing-in questions like these:

— "You mentioned that there were sometimes bottlenecks in shipping goods. How often do they occur?"

— "Do these bottlenecks ever cause delays in delivering goods to your customers? How often?"

— "When customer shipments are delayed, what are the consequences? Do you lose customer good-will? Do you ever have orders cancelled? If so, with what effect on profits? Do you ever lose customers permanently as a result of delayed shipments?"

10. Draw on your expertise in listening for the kind of indicators you should probe in more detail in establishing the Value of filling that need.

If the Prospect admits that there have been difficulties, you can later quote those words back as evidence that the need exists which you can fill.

Further, if you then go on to ask questions relating to Value, you can usually get the Prospect to provide concrete, dollars-and-cents ways in which failing to fill that need is costing money (or costing time or costing inconvenience—which are money under other names).

You can then take those value or cost figures as evidence in showing how your proposed solution can save some of those costs. Thus, those cost-savings can help pay for your services or product.

For example, if your questions regarding the software presently in place turn up that signs that the difficulties result in a lot of wasted time, or inconvenience to customers, or billing errors, you can ask the Prospect to put a cost estimate on each part.

Example (though you would be pausing between each question to listen to the response):

"About how often does the system go down because of software difficulties? For how long? And when it does, what is it costing for each hour of downtime, in areas such as wasted employee time, lost sales, and the like?"

11. Be open to fresh input: the actual needs may be different than you expect.

It's important not only to ask the right questions, but to listen to the responses—and that means not just listening for what you expect to hear, but also for what the customer is really saying. They may open up whole new areas of potential uses or markets for your product.

12. Remember: Ask, don't tell.

It's essential to ask the questions and to listen well to the Prospect's responses for two reasons, both equally important. First, to help you understand this Prospect's need. Second, to help the Prospect understand the need and the implications that flow.

You may be convinced that you already know what the Prospect needs. (In the software example above, you may have known as soon as you heard that this particular product was in use there what the probable needs were, and how you could help, because you had done that kind of work for a dozen other clients.) But ask the questions regardless, for the needs here just might be different.

Even more importantly, though you understand the needs that flow, the Prospect does not.

To repeat the point made earlier: You could tell the Prospect of the needs (but she might only half-listen, just the way you half-listen when someone tells you to eat your spinach because it's good for you). By asking the right questions, you lead the Prospect to tell you, in her own words, what the difficulties are.

Then, once that need is out in the open, then you can move on to explain how you or your product can fill those needs. And, very important, you can quote back the Prospect's own words, making the case for filling the need.

13. The Prospect's overview may provide you several areas of potential need. Focus-in on each of these in turn, then go on to develop Value for those that seem most promising for you.

14. In some cases, it may happen that you Focus-in and develop Value for one area of potential need for your product, then recycle back and Focus-in on other need areas.

Supplement: Checklists of sample questions

The checklists that follow will get you started with some sample questions of each type. Adapt them to your specific product and industry. Expand on the checklists by adding other questions that you find helpful in opening up the discussion.

Overview Questions (after first setting the context by explaining why you are asking these questions):

- I'd appreciate your giving me a brief overview of the work here in the department, particularly as it relates to (whatever your area of interest is).

- I realize that you're the order processing section for the firm, but could you give me a quick tour of the actual flow of the work?

- I'm familiar with the kind of work done in shipping departments generally, but it would help if you could orient me to the specific kinds of projects that flow through your particular section?

Focusing-in Questions:

- You mentioned that you had been having difficulties lately with _____. I'd be interested in hearing more about that.

- When that happens, what kind of impact does it have on the rest of the section? On other departments within the organization? On your relations with customers?

- Do you ever have any difficulties with _____? (You might ask a more pointed question like this if nothing emerges spontaneously.)

- Looking to the future, what areas are you looking to improve or upgrade? (This is another question you can use if no need area emerges, or if the Prospect's responses are too vague to be helpful.)

Value Questions:

- About how often do these difficulties occur?

- When they do occur, what kinds of costs and other impacts result, including direct costs (wasted materials, overtime, etc.), and indirect costs (such as upsetting work schedules in this department and other areas)?

- Can you estimate what the dollar impacts are?

- If you could eliminate (or even reduce) the instances of that happening, what would it be worth to you--in dollar savings?

> In reduced stress? In customer good-will? Can you put a rough dollar figure on each of these?

Summary: Consultative selling: sell by asking smart questions

1. In your work with the Prospect, view your role as that of a consultant working to analyze and solve problems, not just to "push" one particular solution.

2. Important: before asking any questions, begin by setting the context for those questions.

3. Your opening question will usually involve asking the Prospect to give you a brief overview of the relevant area. Your follow-on specific questions will flow from the potential areas of need suggested by that overview (combined with your knowledge of what to look for, given what kinds of needs your product is designed to fill).

4. In asking the questions, it's usually best to work from broad to specific. That is, first developing context, then focusing in on areas of potential need, and only then on the value of filling those needs.

5. OVERVIEW: begin with OVERVIEW questions asking the Prospect to give you broad perspective on the situation and context.

6. FOCUS-IN: once some possible need areas open up, ask Focusing-in questions that build from what has turned up and invite the Prospect to provide more detail on the specific needs that may exist.

7. VALUE: Finally, ask Value questions to lead the Prospect to provide specific information—usually in terms of dollars—that establish

-what the need is costing (directly or indirectly), and,

-the value of filling that need.

8. As the Prospect provides the overview, listen for the indicators that suggest there may be potential need. Focus-in on these for more detail.

9. Since you are already an expert in what your product (or service) can do, you begin with a good idea of what you are looking for, and hence for where your questions should lead.

10. Use your expertise as a mental checklist to guide in listening for the kind of indicators to probe for in establishing the Value of filling that need.

11. But be open to fresh input: the actual needs may be different than you expect.

12. Remember: Ask, don't tell.

13. The Prospect's overview may provide you several areas of potential need. Focus-in on each of these in turn, then go on to develop Value for those that seem most promising for you.

14. In some cases, it may happen that you Focus-in and develop Value for one area of potential need for your product, then recycle back and Focus-in on other need areas.

Step 11: MAKING CLEAR THE LINK BETWEEN THE PROSPECT'S NEEDS AND HOW YOUR PRODUCT (OR SERVICE) WILL FILL THOSE NEEDS

Earlier, we examined how—typically by a question-and-answer dialogue— you and the Prospect can come to a shared awareness of what if any needs exist.

Here you take the next step, making the link between that need (or multiple needs) and the specific ways that your product or service can fill those needs.

1. **In presenting your product (or service), relate it to the SPECIFIC NEEDS of this UNIQUE Prospect.**

Your product may be useful in a dozen ways. But what really matters is how well it fills the specific, identified needs of this Prospect or organization. That is, those particular needs that you and the Prospect have discussed and agreed upon earlier.

Typically, in your dialogue with the Prospect (as in the previous Steps) you may have uncovered one, two, maybe three main needs. Now, as you introduce your product, concentrate on showing how it can fill those key needs.

2. **The more clearly and explicitly you are in making the link between the Prospect's specific needs and the specific ways in which your product fills those needs, the better will be your chances of making the sale.**

In other words, if it develops that this Prospect had significant needs in areas A, C and D, then focus on how your product fills A,

C and D. Don't muddy the waters by saying it also does B, K, L, and M, as well.

Those additional uses (B, K, L, M) may have value, but if you have not established the need for them in the Prospect's mind, they probably are not going to make the sale for you.

These additional uses are a lot like airline Frequent Flyer miles. They may be nice to have, but people buy because they want to get from here to there. Bonus miles are a nice extra, but rarely make or break the sale.

3. **Make the link explicit between the needs you discussed with the Prospect and the specific product capabilities that fill those needs. Don't take for granted that the Prospect sees either the need or the solution as clearly as you do.**

In the course of your dialogue with the Prospect, it may be instantly clear to you that needs exist that your product or service can fill.

But keep in mind that you are an expert both in the capabilities of your product and in the needs it can fill, while the Prospect may be seeing your product for the first time. He may even have only now become aware of those needs, as well as how worthwhile it will be to fill them.

Summarize the key needs you uncovered in your dialogue with the Prospect, then match each need with a capability of your product or service that fills that particular need. The template following provides a model:

Newbie's Guide to Selling Face-to-Face

We discovered these needs . . .	. . . which my product/service can fill in these specific ways:
1.	
2.	

Example:

Suppose you made a sales call on a manufacturing firm. From the discussion, two key needs developed: (1) the need to get the firm's newsletter out on time; and (2) the need to improve the quality of the sales letters being sent out.

Among your many talents, two capabilities match those needs: (1) you have experience in editing newsletters; and (2) you have developed productive sales letters for other clients.

Given that background, here's an example of how you can make that link between the customer's needs and your capabilities:

Review of need #1:

"In our discussion over the past few minutes, you mentioned that you're troubled by the fact that the company's newsletter has been going out a couple of weeks late every month. It seems to be happening because the editor is often tied up with responsibilities for other sections within the company."

Matching your capability to need #2:

"In that regard, I'd like to point out my experience as a free-lance editor of newsletters, and I have some samples I'll show you in a moment."

4. **It's helpful if you can both tell *and* show. Visual aids are strong selling tools, as they can help "show."**

There's an old saying to the effect that "Words alone cannot describe," and another about a picture being worth a thousand words. Selling is communicating, and a simple visual aid can often communicate the point better than words alone ever could.

Look back now at the mental template in item 3, above. You can adapt that as a simple visual aid which you can hand-print on a piece of note-paper while you're sitting with the Prospect. List the key needs in one column, and the capabilities that enable you to fill each need in the column beside it. Example:

Your needs:	How I (my product or service) can help:
Late newsletters	As outside editor, I can devote as much or as little time that is needed.
Weak sales letters	Draw from my experience in developing effective sales letters for other organizations.

5. **If it then develops that the Prospect is not ready to buy on the basis of how your product can fill these first needs, then RECYCLE back to explore other areas of possible need.**

In your discussion with the Prospect, you may pick up indicators of several areas of potential need for your product. You can't talk about everything first, so begin by focusing on one or two.

If those make the sale for you, fine. If not, recycle back, reviewing other needs that you uncovered, and showing how you can fill them.

6. **Be attuned to signals that indicate that the Prospect wants additional proof.**

7. **But before offering any kind of proof, make certain that both you and the Prospect are in accord on exactly what needs to be proven.**

Your claim that your service or your product can fill the Prospect's needs may not alone be convincing enough, and may need to be supplemented by proof.

What kind of proof to offer depends on the unique interests of the Prospect (here abbreviated as P), as well as what precisely what is in doubt. The chart following offers guidance:

If you encounter . . .	that probably means . . .	so offer proof of this sort:
. . . indicators that P is not convinced that the need is serious or urgent.	You were too quick in moving on from developing the needs in your dialogue with P. Or, you did not touch upon high-priority needs.	Review the needs you uncovered earlier. Review what failing to fill these needs is costing the Prospect and firm. Or, offer to do a no-cost/low-cost needs analysis in more detail.
. . . indicators that P is not convinced that your service or product can in fact fill the need/do the job.	You "talked" about your capability, but P needs to "see" it with own eyes.	Maybe offer a free sample, or a free demonstration. Or, arrange testimonials from other satisfied customers.
. . . indicators that P does not take you seriously.	Doubts about your experience or ability to bring about practical, real-world results.	Improve the professionalism of your appearance, letterheads, brochures, etc.

Proof may also take the form of free samples, reduced-cost introductory offers, or short-term, no obligation trials.

But be cautious about giving freebies and discounts, as there are—can you believe it!— free-loaders who'll take undue advantage of your offer.

If you're a consultant, free-agent, or other kind of "idea-worker," you need to tread carefully: you do need to offer some details of what you will do, and how you will proceed. But you also need to be aware of the risk that some clients will capture your expertise and accomplish it with in-house staff, or take the "education" you have given and go to someone else to see if they will do it for less money.

Additional forms of proof

Beyond those mentioned here, additional ways of providing proof to Prospects include:

- Written proposals (which may focus on issues such as cost, starting or ending date, and the like);

- Demonstrations of your product in action;

- Formal presentations, perhaps to the decision team;

- Trial offers. But, again, beware: before giving "freebies," get a commitment on just what that trial is to prove, and what happens when that proof source proves your case: in most cases, that should be their up-front agreement to buy if you proven your case. In most cases, if they are not willing to make that agreement in advance, then it's usually not worth your proceeding with the proof, be it a written proposal, demo, or whatever.

Each of these proof sources have their proper place, but before investing your time and energy, make sure that you and the Prospect are in agreement both on what is to be proven, and what happens next: that if you prove the points agreed upon up-front, that the Prospect will buy.

For more on proof sources, as well as how to obtain that up-front agreement with the Prospect see my book, **Sales Presentations and Demonstrations**. You'll find more how-to at my site: http://sales-training-source.com/

Newbie's Guide to Selling Face-to-Face

Summary: Making the link between the Prospect's needs and how your product will fill those needs

1. In presenting your product (or service), relate it to the SPECIFIC NEEDS of this UNIQUE Prospect.

2. The more specific you are in making the link between specific needs and the specific ways in which your product fills those needs, the better will be your chances of making the sale.

3. Make the link explicit between the needs you discussed with the Prospect and the specific product capabilities that fill those needs. Don't take for granted that the Prospect sees either the need or the solution as clearly as you do.

4. It's helpful to both tell and show. Visual aids are strong selling tools.

5. If it then develops that the Prospect is not ready to buy on the basis of how your product can fill these first needs, then RECYCLE back to explore other areas of possible need.

6. Be attuned to signals that indicate that the Prospect wants additional proof.

7. But before offering any kind of proof, make certain that you and the Prospect are in accord on exactly what needs to be proven.

Michael McGaulley

Step 12: WHEN DEALING WITH THE ISSUE OF PRICE, FOCUS ON "VALUE"

1. The question of cost will naturally be in the Prospect's mind.

2. But much more important than cost is "value"-- that is, what the Prospect will gain in exchange for the money spent.

3. Therefore, to make the sale, you need to shift the Prospect's thinking from a narrow focus on price (the money spent), to the broader issue of value (whether and why that is a worthwhile investment).

Think of it this way: it's tough to part with a dollar, but it makes perfect sense to spend that dollar if you get back $1.25 or, better, $2.00 in value for each $1.00 you spend.

Part of your role as a sales person is to point out the ways in which the Prospect gets back clear value for the money invested in your service or product.

Put differently, if your product is good, and if it is needed badly enough, the Prospect will probably buy.

4. But if you can also show that the product will help pay for itself, by value received, then the reasons for buying become almost overwhelming. It is up to you to help the Prospect understand all the ways in which your product or service brings value greater than what the price may be.

> **5. If you're new to selling, the thought of mentioning price is scary, and you may be tempted to put it off as long as possible.**

After all, you have invested time and energy in this call, and you may feel you don't want to risk wasting all that effort. So you are tempted to put off speaking of cost until later . . . and later.

Wrong move, because . . .

> **6. If you wait for the customer to ask about the price, then you operate from a disadvantage, and . . .**

> **7. It's best to deal with price at a time that is best for you, so you can address dollars in context of the benefits it brings.**

The best time to speak of money will usually be after you have both, established the Prospect's needs, and linked those needs with the specific ways in which your product or service can fill them.

That way, you can present price in context. Thus it becomes a matter not of the cost, but rather an investment in filling a recognized need. Address dollars from a positive perspective, not a defensive status.

> **8. To enhance the Prospect's awareness of the value of your product, first set context by briefly reviewing both,**
>
> **--the needs uncovered, and,**
>
> **--the specific ways in which your product will fill those needs.**

Here's an example of how those aspects work together.

First, establishing value by reviewing the discussion of needs and how they can be filled:

"As we discussed, your firm is facing four major needs at the moment, all of which, we agreed, relate to the need to upgrade the specialized software used in your computers. As I have pointed out, each of these four needs can be filled by key features of my firm's software package, EFFICIENCY PLUS. We also found that the present cost of these unfilled needs totals over $3,000 for each month. By filling these needs, you gain $3,000 per month, for a total saving of $36,000 in a year's time."

Then addressing value in different terms:

"Therefore, I think you'll agree with me that EFFICIENCY PLUS, which costs $24,000 installed, is an investment that will pay for itself within eight months of the time we install it here."

Finally, "Closing" for the order:

"Given your approval today, it can be operational here as of the first of the month. It makes good business sense to begin filling these needs as soon as possible, don't you think?"

In that example, notice that the transition from speaking of cost (and value) to asking (or "closing") for the order was seamless. We'll focus on closing in the following Step.

9. After presenting price, immediately move on . . . usually by closing for the order (or for some other kind of buying action).

Once you have stated price, you don't want to let the dollar figure hang in the air, growing and growing in a vacuum. Usually, the best way to move on is to ask (or "close") for the order, as in the example just above.

If you have established the background—that is, what the Prospect's needs are, and how your product can fill those needs—then you are justified in assuming that the investment makes sense. If what you propose makes good business sense, then it is only logical to work on the assumption that the Prospect will naturally elect to buy.

Looking at it another way: if you present price and then pause to hear the Prospect's reaction, then you stop the momentum of the sale.

Instead, present price, then immediately move to ask for the order.

If the Prospect has questions about the cost, or about anything else, you can be sure that she will stop you and bring you back to deal with those issues. Unless and until the Prospect says otherwise, keep the momentum going.

About that term, "other kind of buying action": it all depends on the situation and what you're selling. Sometimes it is reasonable to wrap up with a signed order. But other times the appropriate "buying action" might be for the Prospect to agree to come into your showroom, or to agree to a short-term trial, or whatever is appropriate to advance the process at that stage.

10. The terms you use to express value will depend on the Prospect, the needs, and various other factors in the situation.

Thus "Value" can take the form of money saved, of time saved, of greater convenience or flexibility, of raised capabilities, or of anything else that happens to be significant to this Prospect.

In most of the examples so far, we have focused on showing how "value" reflects dollar savings—that is, how your product can pay for itself in direct savings.

But you can also express value in ways other than dollar savings.

- For some Prospects, that sense of value may come if you can enable them to bypass certain tasks so they can focus on the work they prefer or consider most important. For example, a sensible business-person will be very pleased to pay $1000 to a tax service if that saves a week's effort, and particularly if she can use that saved time to bring in new business worth five or ten times that amount.

- Similarly, larger firms may contract out certain services to specialized firms or contractors in order to avoid the overhead of doing the work in-house. There the value may come from the cost-savings of not needing to keep a specialist on staff.

- Smaller organizations may contract out for the sake of the time savings that result from not having to learn how to do a new task, thereby allowing the person to concentrate on doing what they do best. (It takes a lot of time and effort to keep climbing up new learning curves!)

- If you are selling a labor-saving tool, for example, you might express the savings in either of two ways: "It saves the costs of having to add extra staff," or, "It frees your staff so they can spend more time developing new business."

11. Another way to make the value clear: break down overall cost into smaller units, or into something of greater meaning to the Prospect.

An ad for a car-rental company states the weekly price for an upgrade car, then breaks that down to how little more that better car will cost per day, then breaks it down further to make the point that there is a relatively small difference in cost per hour or per rental to drive in luxury.

You may be able to adapt the strategy. Suppose that you are selling a product that costs $1,000 more than your competitor's. To minimize that gap, point out that over the estimated five-year useful life of the product, that extra $1,000 spent on your unit works out to only about 80 cents per day, (given that there are roughly 250 working days in each of the five years it will be in service).

12. Still another way of establishing the value: combine multiple ways in which the product either pays for itself or makes life easier, more convenient, or adds more hours to the day.

13. Refer to incidental uses as a way of increasing the customer's perception of the value of your product.

Back in Step 11, I suggested that you focus your discussion on the specific ways in which your product can fill the specific needs that came up in the course of your dialogue with the Prospect. The point was that a scatter-shot discussion of elements that don't link to those needs probably will do you more harm than good. They may only confuse, without adding to buying interest.

But now, as you try to pile up additional "value" to nudge the customer the final inch to yes, it generally is productive to raise these secondary benefits. Example:

"We spoke earlier of the four key needs you face this year, and of how my product can fill those needs. But that's by no means all the product can do for you. For instance, it can _____, and it can _____. Indeed, another firm like yours in Plainsburg found a novel use that not even we, the developers, had anticipated. That suggests how flexible a tool it will be once you install it here."

But keep in mind that incidental uses are only that — *incidental*, not essential

Once again, base the main thrust of your selling approach on matching specific features of your product to specific needs the customer faces. At that point, don't clutter up your selling message by digressing into other uses of your product for which you have not laid a foundation by highlighting specific needs those features can fill.

However, at a later point in the selling cycle when you are establishing all of the ways in which the product can help pay for itself, then it is appropriate to refer to these additional features or capabilities of your product.

At that point, these additional capabilities become "extras" that might help nudge the decision to yes, or nudge the decision toward you rather than a competitor.

But it's important that you don't get bogged down on these additional features and uses. You don't want to confuse the issue for the customer. The point you are making at this point is to the effect that,

"... not only will it largely pay for itself in the ways I have pointed out, but beyond that has even greater potential for repaying the investment via these additional features."

Summary: Dealing with the issue of price: talk "value"

1. The question of cost will naturally be in the Prospect's mind.

2. But much more important than cost is "value"– that is, what will be gained in return for the money spent.

3. Therefore, to make the sale, you need to shift the Prospect's thinking from a narrow focus on price (the money spent), to the broader issue of value (whether and why that is a worthwhile investment).

4. If you're new to selling, the thought of mentioning price may be scary, something you may be inclined to put off as long as possible.

5. But if you wait for the customer to ask about the price, then you operate from a disadvantage.

6. It's better to deal with price at the time that is best for you, so you can address it from a positive perspective, in context of the needs filled and the benefits gained, rather than being on the defensive about it.

7. To enhance the Prospect's awareness of the value of your product, briefly review both the needs uncovered as well as the specific ways in which your product will fill those needs.

8. After presenting price, immediately move on . . . usually by closing for the order.

9. The terms you use to express value will depend on the Prospect, the needs, and various other factors in the situation.

10. Another way to make the value clear: break down overall cost into smaller units, or into something of greater meaning to the Prospect.

11. Still another way of establishing the value: combine multiple ways in which the product either pays for itself or makes life easier, more convenient, or adds more hours to the day.

12. Refer to incidental uses as a way of increasing the customer's perception of the value of your product. (But keep in mind that incidental uses are only that—incidental, not essential.)

Michael McGaulley

Step 13: BEING ATTUNED TO "BUYING SIGNALS"

We'll be focusing on "closing" in the next Step. What is closing? Basically, it's "closing up the sale." That may mean asking for the order, or may mean asking the Prospect to take some kind of buying action toward the next step. Perhaps that action may be agreeing to attend a presentation, to sit in on a demonstration of your product in action, or to assent to a trial run.

Before getting into the how-to of closing, let's take a look at buying signals, which are the small clues the Prospect may send—sometimes intentionally, sometimes unconsciously—that she is ready to be closed.

1. The "right" time to close can come at any time in the call; hence, be alert for buying signals.

We're examining the how-to of closing at this point in the book because that is the "logical" place to close—after establishing the needs, and showing how your product fills those needs.

But a sales call may have its own logic, and the best time to close may come much earlier in the call — earlier, in short, than you might expect.

In some cases, the right time to close might be very close to the time you begin, if the Prospect shows buying signals that indicate that level of interest.

What are "buying signals?" We'll examine some common types in this Step.

2. Buying signals are often conveyed by the Prospect's questions.

You can often gauge the Prospect's degree of interest by the questions she asks. People generally don't ask certain kinds of questions *unless* they are seriously considering buying. Typical buying signal questions include:

- *"What does it cost?"* (Unless the Prospect is just naturally curious, interest in cost signals overall interest.)

- "Is it available in (a particular color, size, model, etc.)?"

- *"How soon can you deliver?"* (That suggests an immediate need.)

- "What warranty comes with it?

3. Before answering a question, "look through" to determine whether that question may be a buying signal.

In deciphering whether a question is a buying signal, consider what the question implies, as well as why they are asking that question at that time.

For instance, a person who has no real interest in your product usually isn't going to bother asking what it costs, or whether it is available in sea-foam green, or how soon they can have delivery.

Which means, if they do ask how soon they can have delivery, hold back on your first impulse, which might be to say something like, "by the first of the month."

Instead, respond to their question with your own related question. Here that might be, "How soon do you need it?"

Why ask? Why not just answer their question? First, because your question in response tests how serious they are in asking that question.

Second, your question sets up for the close: "Will it meet your needs if we can install by the first of the month?" If they say yes, then wrap up the sale. If they hesitate, find why, then deal with that as an objection.

4. Even objections and tough questions may be buying signals.

A customer who objects, "We couldn't possibly think about buying a new system now, not when we're coming into our busy season," is indirectly signaling interest in buying under certain conditions implied in the question/objection.

If you "look through" that objection—"We can't buy now, not when we're coming into our busy season"—you might discern that their real concern is reliability: they don't want to risk testing out something new in the busy season.

That suggests two possibilities for you. First, they've signaled that they'll be ready to buy after the busy season. Or, second, it may signal that the sale can be made now, provided you can overcome their concerns about the reliability of a new product.

How do you uncover a Prospect's real concerns?

Sometimes they will be apparent if you're attuned to facial expressions and other non-verbals, or if you listen to what is really being said behind the Prospect's questions or comments.

Other times, you'll need to ask questions that help the Prospect pull into words what may be a vague feeling:

"Ms. Prospect, you say 'not now when we're coming into our busy season.' Why would you want to wait? Do you have a concern about the reliability of the product?"

Similarly, a customer who says, *"Your competitor has a great product, especially in its _____ capability,"* is signaling—consciously or not—that he has given some thought to the need, and has determined which criteria are particularly important. Therefore, focus on showing how your product is better than the competitor against the criteria cited by the Prospect.

5. When you encounter a question or objection that may be a buying signal, respond to it, then immediately transition to a trial close.

Here's an example of attempting a test close on the heels of a response to an objection. First, the response to the objection:

"You're right, the Whizco's RER feature has been the standard of the industry. But only until now. Now our new Ultima is setting a new standard. Where the Whizco would take two hours to accomplish the task that you speak of, and with a five-percent error rate, the Ultima can accomplish the same task in approximately half the time, with zero errors. But don't just take my word for it. Advanced Industries replaced all of their Whizco units last year with new Ultimas, and the results are even better than they projected."

Then an immediate transition from the response to a trial close:

"Mr. Wadsworth at Advanced has indicated that he is so pleased with what the Ultima has done for his firm that he invites Prospective Ultima purchasers to visit his office and see the units in action. I'd like to set up a visit for you. Would you like to do that perhaps an afternoon later this week, or would early next week be better?"

In this example, notice how the close was not for the order itself, because in this situation that would be too big a step at one time. Instead, the salesperson asked the Prospect to take the interim step of committing some time and effort to view a demonstration.

> **6. A Prospect who shows interest in negotiating (or haggling over details) is usually sending a strong buying signal.**

"Is that the best price you can give me?," or, "What volume discounts are available?," or, "How soon can you install?" are all signals that the Prospect may be ready to buy.

After all, people normally don't ask these kinds of questions unless they are seriously interested—interested, at least, to the degree that cost or delivery times matter to them.

> **7. Buying signals may be non-verbal.**

A Prospect who is sitting forward in the chair, head vigorously nodding, eyes sparkling with interest is sub-consciously radiating a high level of interest. It's probably a good time to fast-forward from wherever you happen to be in the sales call in order to attempt to close for the order (or whatever other buying action is appropriate in that case).

There's nothing particularly exotic about non-verbal buying signals; you're probably already familiar with many of them from everyday experience. Here are a few to get you started; expand the checklist as others come to you.

- *Facial expression*: a Prospect who looks bored and distracted is probably not sending buying signals. (No surprise there.) But a Prospect whose face is animated, with eyes alert and focused on you or your product is at least interested, perhaps even ready to the extent of being ready to buy.

- *Proximity:* a Prospect who leans forward, toward either you or the product, is signaling a rising level of interest. If you are standing beside someone who has been "keeping his distance," and then he turns or moves more toward you, read that as a signal of increasing interest, and perhaps even of buying interest.

Caution: we are conditioned to keep a "circle of personal space" around us.

If someone moves into that space, we tend to draw back to keep the personal space circle intact.

But if a sales Prospect comes toward you, resist the impulse to move back. A Prospect's coming toward you (or your product) is usually a good sign, a sign of interest. Stay forward so you can literally "get your heads together."

8. Rule of thumb regarding possible buying signals: If in doubt, test it out.

That is, if you seem to be getting what appears to be a buying signal (though aren't completely sure), it may be a good time to attempt a trial close.

If the Prospect goes for the close, then you can write up the order. If not, resume from where you left off.

9. Don't be compulsive about "finishing" everything in your planned sales call: seize opportunities if they arise.

If the Prospect sends out buying signals before you have finished all that you had planned to say, pause in your coverage to test that interest by a trial close.

Newbie's Guide to Selling Face-to-Face

If the trial close goes well, you may have no need to continue making your case. You may be able to write up the order.

Conversely, if it turns out that the Prospect is not yet ready to buy, then you lost nothing by the trial close. Simply transition back to where you were, and carry on with the points you were making a moment earlier.

Summary: Attuning to buying signals

1. The "right" time to close can come at any time in the call; hence, be alert for buying signals.

2. Buying signals are often conveyed by the Prospect's questions.

3. Before answering a question, first "look through" to determine whether that question may be a buying signal.

4. Even objections and tough questions may be buying signals.

5. When you encounter a question or objection that may be a buying signal, respond to it, then immediately transition to a trial close.

6. A Prospect who shows interest in negotiating (or haggling over details) is usually sending a strong buying signal.

7. Buying signals may be non-verbal.

8. Rule of thumb regarding possible buying signals: If in doubt, test it out.

9. Don't be compulsive about "finishing" everything in your planned sales call: seize opportunities to close early if they arise

Michael McGaulley

Step 14: CLOSING FOR THE ORDER, OR FOR OTHER TYPES OF "BUYING ACTION"

There's no single best way of asking (or "closing") for an order or other kind of buying action. Use whatever feels comfortable and natural to you under the circumstances.

This Step will introduce you to four basic methods to get you started. Add others later as your experience builds, or as you feel the need to expand your repertoire of closing approaches.

1. **Simple direct request for the order (or other buying action).**

Summarize the key needs along with how your product or service will fill those needs, then ask for the order.

First the summary:

"We discussed the difficulties you've been experiencing in the _____ department, resulting in delayed shipment of customer orders. You mentioned how the delays cost some customer goodwill, resulting in what you estimated at a one-percent rate of cancelled orders. I showed you how the software package developed by my firm will address those bottlenecks, reducing shipment delays, which should virtually eliminate orders cancelled by unhappy customers. You estimated that reducing those cancellations alone would save the company at least $1,000 per month. All of these factors add up to one basic point: when you install my package, you're going to begin shipping with fewer delays, and the package will pay for itself within the first nine months."

Then the close:

"Your authorization today means that we can have it in place by the first of this coming month. I think you'll agree that's a good business decision."

2. Summary and Recommendations: summarize the key reasons to buy, then recommend that the Prospect act now.

Again, briefly summarize the various needs that you have discussed with the Prospect, along with the ways in which your product (or service) fills each of those needs,

In some cases, you might also ask the Prospect to confirm whether you have covered all of the key points, perhaps by asking a question like, "Is there anything we need to talk about now?"

If yes, deal with it. If no, then immediately move on to ask for the order. Example:

First the summary:

"Recapping what we've covered, your group has been hampered by a series of situations in which your newsletter has been late in getting out, mainly because your in-house editor is overburdened with duties to another division of the company. I showed you some of the newsletters I produce for other clients, and you seemed quite pleased with what you saw. If you call my other client contacts, you'll find that I have a reputation of making deadlines.

"A second topic we discussed was your dissatisfaction with the sales letters that have been going out on your firm's letterhead. You seemed quite excited by some of the sample letters I showed you.

"You estimated that because your present letters aren't as effective as they could be, you're losing perhaps ten percent of sales, which translates into about $500 per month in profit.

"Given my experience, I can help you with both needs. That is, in making your sales letters more productive, and in getting the newsletter out on time."

Then the close, via a recommendation:

"The deadline for the March issue of the newsletter is only ten days away, but I can commit to making that deadline, given your go-ahead today. I can also take some of your present sales letters with me today, and begin work immediately revising them, so you can have the improved versions ready for your mailing next month. That would mean that you can begin boosting your profits that much sooner. I think it makes good business sense to move quickly, do you agree?"

3. Offer a Choice of Alternatives for implementing your proposed solution.

Instead of asking the Prospect to buy, or to agree to the dates on an action plan, here you propose a pair of alternatives from which the Prospect can choose.

For the sales person, the art comes in presenting two alternatives structured so that a yes to either implies a yes to the sale.

The shop clerk who asks, "Will you be paying with cash or credit card?" is using the choice of alternatives as a way of closing the sale.

Note that the clerk is not asking "Do you want to buy?," but is instead asking, "Which method do you want to use in order to pay?" Regardless of whether you say "cash" or "credit card," your response implies "Yes, I'll buy."

Similarly, the salesperson who asks, "Do you prefer the Dusty Rose or the Sea Foam Green?" is setting up another subtle alternative choice. True, you might "prefer" the green without intending to buy anything, but that's not the way the question works.

Once you've indicated that your preference is green (or rose, it doesn't matter), then the sales person's alternate choice question will be whether you prefer to take it with you or have it shipped, and then whether you prefer the regular or extended warranty. Then will come the alternatives of "Would you prefer the extended warranty?" (Which implies the unspoken alternative of the regular warranty.) And so forth.

Whether or not to use the alternate choice approach

Use the Choice of Alternatives as a closing tool only if you are comfortable with it, as your discomfort would be perceptible to the Prospect.

If you do use the approach, it's essential to plan out in advance—and rehearse—the alternatives you present. Setting up two useful alternatives which both imply the same ultimate conclusion is not something you can improvise on the spot.

At least get clearly in your mind the mental framework of how you will word the alternatives, then rehearse until the words flow smoothly and comfortably. You can then fill in the blanks on the spot, with the specific alternatives of time, color, or whatever.

Developing the pattern of offering alternative choices

Alternative choice as a method of closing for the order works best when you've prepared the way by setting up a pattern of previous alternatives.

That is, your setting up the alternatives that imply yes to the sale will flow more naturally if you have, throughout the call, been presenting the Prospect with other alternatives from which to choose.

You may have presented the first pair of alternatives earlier when you were arranging the meeting: "Would it be better to meet late this week or early next? Are mornings or afternoons generally better for you?"

You can pose other alternatives through the call, such as,

"My firm can arrange to dispose of the used cartridges for you, or we can recommend a firm that does that work on contract. Would you rather have us do it, or would you prefer to arrange that separately?"

Or you might propose,

"It would be helpful for me to have a brief overview of the flow of the work here, so that I can better target my comments today. Do you think it would be more efficient for us to walk through the operation, or can we do that from here in your office?"

4. Offer a proposed Action Plan.

Again, as above, summarize the needs and your proposed solutions. Then, instead of directly asking for the order, propose an Action Plan, setting out the details of specific steps to be taken, along with "milestone" dates for each. (If the idea of an Action

Plan doesn't seem to fit your situation, you might refer to it as an "Implementation Schedule.")

An advantage of the Action Plan approach: it skips over the question of whether or not to buy, and shifts the Prospect's attention to the details of implementing your proposal. Example:

The first three paragraphs are the same as in the example above, then,

"You said that your March newsletter needs to go in the mail on February the twentieth. To make that deadline, I'll need all copy from the contributors in final form by the fifteenth. My first step will be to notify each contributors of the delivery deadline, along with suggested topics to cover. That's the action plan I suggest, and I know I can work within it. Does it seem feasible to you? If that's agreeable, then I'll start on it immediately as soon as we finalize the details."

Using a written Action Plan as a tool for closing

In the example above, the Action Plan was improvised on the spot, and presented orally.

But the Action Plan approach can be even more powerful if you can put the plan on paper. If you have the good fortune of possessing legible handwriting, you could draft the Action Plan on a notepad while you are with the Prospect.

(If you do either a verbal or handwritten action plan, and the Prospect agrees, then type it up and send it to the Prospect as soon as possible to confirm your mutual understandings.)

Better yet: prepare the proposed written Action Plan in advance

In some cases, you can prepare a typed Proposed Action Plan to bring into the meeting. This is particularly feasible when you're making a second call on a Prospect.

However, if your recommendations tend to fall into predictable patterns, you may be able to go into even first calls with a draft Action Plan in hand. You can work out any modifications, then pencil them in on the spot.

Even if you begin the call knowing that some changes will be necessary in the draft Action Plan, the plan still serves a useful purpose. For one thing, the proposed plan helps focus the discussion by pinning myriad issues down into a sequence of concrete steps and dates.

Further, by using the draft Action Plan as a discussion topic, you'll find that the Prospect's focus typically shifts from the question of whether to buy, to the more promising (for you) question of whether these are realistic dates for implementing the new system.

Other Methods of Closing for the Sale

These four methods will get you started. (At the start, it's better to master a limited number of approaches than to be overwhelmed and uncomfortable with more than you can handle.)

Key point: Once you close for the sale (whichever approach you use), stop talking. Let the power of silence work for you.

Regardless of how you ask for the sale, once you ask . . . stop talking.

Be silent from that moment . . . because once you ask, the ball lands in the Prospect's court. Leave it there and let the Prospect figure out what to do about it.

However, be prepared for the difficulty you may have in holding that silence. We humans are conditioned to find silence intimidating. Unless you're an unusual sort, you'll probably want to intervene in the silence, and say something to ease the pressure.

But understand that you're not alone in finding that silence intimidating. At least you are prepared for the silence, because you knew it was coming.

Besides, you have said your piece, and now it's up to the other person to respond. You have done your part by asking; now the Prospect has the power to end that silence by responding.

Chances are they will say something, anything, just to ease the pressure. They may say, "Yes, I want it!" Or they may say No, or may blurt out the first reason that comes to their mind for not buying.

If they say yes, then that makes it easy.

But regardless of what they say, recognize that it is useful feedback on what they are actually thinking about you, your product, and the idea of buying. Once you have that feedback—and the pressure of silence fosters brutal honesty—you can respond in a targeted manner, focusing on the specific issue that's foremost in their mind.

The silence after you ask for the order will normally only last for a few seconds. But it can go longer, for half a minute, for a minute, for even longer.

Newbie's Guide to Selling Face-to-Face

If you break that silence, you lose the opportunity to get the Prospect to make a decision. By breaking the silence, you rescue her, and put the burden back on yourself to again ask for the sale.

Summary: Basic closing methods

1. Simple direct request for the order (or other buying action).

2. Summary and Recommendations: summarize the key reasons to buy, then recommend that the Prospect act now.

3. Offer a Choice of Alternatives for implementing your proposed solution.

4. Offer a proposed Action Plan.

Key point: Once you close for the sale, stop talking. Let the power of silence work for you.

Michael McGaulley

Step 15: RESPONDING TO OBJECTIONS AND QUESTIONS

When you hear an objection, it usually seems that the Prospect has decided not to buy. Conversely, when you hear a question, on the other hand, it seems that the Prospect is still interested, and is just seeking more information.

The reality is: objections and questions are often just alternative ways of asking for information.

1. **In many cases, what seems to be an objection is often a question in disguise. Conversely, what seems to be a question may actually be an objection.**

2. **You can *lose* the sale if you don't find out what the customer is thinking *behind the words*.**

Objections and questions may seem to arrive with different intent, but in effect are generally not that different. Oftentimes, the objections you hear either are simply questions being asked in another form, or are requests for you to explain that issue better.

Sometimes an objection really means, You've persuaded me, but I know my boss (or spouse) is going to raise this point, so tell me how to handle it.

An objection may even be a subtle test of how sure you are of your self and your product. Sometimes Prospects may try to take your measure by playing hard-to-get. They may throw out objections, not because these are issues of any great concern to them, but rather as a way of finding out how well you bounce back, which reflects on how confident you are in your product and what it can do.

3. When you hear no, or when you hear an objection, don't fold. Find what the real concern is, then turn it around and use that as a selling point.

If a Prospect says, "I like your product, but it's too expensive," your initial impulse might be to offer a price break.

But that impulse might not be the smartest reaction. First of all, the price break you offer might not get you the sale, because what that Prospect means by too expensive might be something that no discount can cure.

Second, even if the discount you offer does result in the sale, the reality is that you might have given away profit that wasn't necessary.

In short, it's a mistake to concede too quickly, because at the start you can't really know what this Prospect means by too expensive.

- The Prospect may be thinking that the product seems expensive because it costs more than a competitor's seemingly-comparable product.

- The Prospect may mean that it is expensive in the sense that the price is higher than he is authorized to purchase without getting approval from above.

- Or it may be that the product seems expensive because the Prospect is not convinced that the need it fills is worth the cost.

As you see, each of these meanings suggests a different concern, which is why the reflexive offer of a price break may not do the good you hope for.

Similarly, if you explore what a Prospect means by "We can't afford it," you might discover any of the following meanings:

- Maybe they'll say that they can't afford it because they "don't have any money." But is that literally no money at all, so bankruptcy looms? Or is it just no money left in this year or quarter's budget?

- Maybe "can't afford it" really means they don't have money to spare on something that seems unnecessary because they don't feel a strong-enough sense of need for it.

- Maybe they can't afford it because you have failed to show how what you offer will help pay for itself, in either the short or long-term.

- It could be that can't afford it means that your competitor is offering a better price.

- Can't afford it may also be the Prospect's way of testing to see if you will cut your price, or offer better terms.

- Still another possibility: We can't afford it may be code words indicating that your product or service, as you have now packaged the offer, exceeds this Prospect's buying authority. (If you can suggest a way of breaking the sale into parts then it may become affordable.)

These are just a few of the potential meanings behind the common objection, and you won't know which it is (and hence which response to take) unless you ask the right questions to uncover the deeper truth.

However, as you explore the meaning, don't be surprised if you find that the Prospect himself is not consciously aware of the real core of his concern.

Thus as you probe to understand the real meaning behind the objection, you may also help the Prospect unfreeze from a subconscious block to buying. He may respond to nearly everything as too expensive not because it is expensive (in terms of value received), but rather from a fear of spending money.

4. Objections and questions can provide the key to the sale, provided you are able to get through assumptions and facades to explore the real meaning.

Some questions, like some objections, are so simple that you can safely respond directly.

But sometimes even simple questions may give you useful clues to what the Prospect is really thinking. For example, when a Prospect asks, Is your product available in blue? you could answer simply yes or no, and move on.

But they probably had a reason in mind for asking that question. If you can isolate that reason, then perhaps you can turn it around and use it as a selling point. Here's an example of how to do that.

Prospect: Is the product available in blue?

Sales Person: *May I ask why blue is important to you?* (Note that here the sales-person asks a question before answering the Prospect's question. By waiting, the Sales Person gains a better sense of how to answer.)

Prospect: We're planning to redecorate the office next month, and we plan to use blue as a main theme.

Now this sales person knows some interesting things. She knows, first, that the Prospect is giving her product some serious consideration, for otherwise he wouldn't have asked about color.

Second, she knows that availability of the product in blue is apparently one of the key criteria in buying.

If the product is available in blue, it would be easy enough just to say yes. But by first inquiring why blue is important, she gains a way of asking for the order:

Sales person: So you would like to install it, provided I can get it for you in an appropriate shade of blue?

On the other hand, suppose the product does not normally come in blue. If the sales person says that immediately, then that door is closed, and the Prospect may be thinking that blue is crucial.

But if, instead of responding immediately, she asks why blue is important, she may find a way of dealing with it while still staying in the running. Here's one way:

Sales person: Blue is not yet one of our standard colors. However, I may be able to special-order it. How soon will you need delivery?

Note that "How soon will you need delivery?" is a close. If the response is, let's say, "October 1," then that sets up the parameters.

If the Prospect responds, "October 1, but I'm not sure I'm ready to commit yet," then the sales person has an opening to probe to find why they are holding back.

On the other hand, if blue is absolutely unavailable, she could suggest that the "colors we stock might offer a nice contrast to the blue theme you already have in place."

5. The model approach in responding to objections and questions: Explore, Listen Well, Restate (if appropriate), Respond, then Move on.

- **Explore**. Ask questions to get the person talking about what they really mean by the objection, and why it's important to them. (Why do you feel that way? will do if nothing better comes to mind.)

- **Listen well** to the response. You may have heard this objection a dozen times already this week, but this person may put a different twist on it. Don't be too quick in cutting off the Prospect's response in order to interject your response. The more you know about the Prospect's needs and mindset the better you can target your response. Sometimes, the Prospect will actually respond to her own concern, and say something like, Never mind, I think I've answered myself. That's really not so important, after all.

- **Restate, if appropriate**. In many cases, it can be helpful to both yourself and the Prospect to paraphrase your understanding of the core of the Prospect's response. For one thing, it forces you to listen closely, so you can restate it clearly. Second, it forces the Prospect to listen to you in turn, to ensure that your restatement is accurate. Further, in some cases, by restating, you may be able to defuse, or take the edge off, the customer's concern.

- **Respond to what they have actually said**. There may be a deeper meaning behind the objection, so focus on that. Example:

"You say that your firm has already tried using consultants, and isn't interested. But I'm picking up a deeper message that your dissatisfaction was with the work of one particular consulting firm that didn't work out for you. I'd like to explain how . . ."

- **Move on from there**; don't get bogged down in your response. Respond to the objection, then go on with your sales call.

If you say too much in response to an objection, you may blow it up into something larger and more significant than the Prospect originally had in mind. If you bog down on it, repeating and elaborating your reaction, the Prospect will think this really must be a major concern, and take that as a reason not to buy.

Conversely, if you treat the objection as a small issue not very important, you are send the subliminal message is that it is just that— minor, not a significant concern, not an issue that could possibly stop the sale.

6. **Rule of thumb: if, when you explore an objection, you find that the Prospect's reasons keeps shifting, or the Prospect keeps raising additional objections, that indicates that you have not yet cut to the core of the real concern.**

Suppose the Prospect first objects on cost grounds, and you deal with that. Then he objects that your product is the wrong color, and you handle that satisfactorily. Then he objects that it won't fit into the space available, or doesn't offer the kind of service he needs. You go on to handle those objections, and then he raises something else.

Sometimes, one objection might lead to a second, and the second might lead to a third.

But if it goes much beyond that, that's usually a sign that you're dealing with something more fundamental than specific issues.

You need to dig deeper to find the real, ultimate concern. Here's an example of how to do that:

"You've raised a series of concerns, and I think I've dealt with each to your satisfaction. But my experience tells me that when I encounter this many concerns, there's usually a deeper issue in the background, which the purchaser may not even be consciously aware of. I think it would help us both if we spent a few moments looking to see what that deeper concern is might be."

The power of silence when you close

Once you have said that, stop talking, and let the power of silence work for you. In that silence, the Prospect may blurt out what's really bothering him.

If that doesn't happen, then you may need to be more direct in your probes, and ask, "Is there a problem with the product itself?," or, "Is there someone else who should be sitting in with us?"

Listen to the response, but listen also to what is unsaid behind it, because when a Prospect throws out a flurry of objections that's usually a sign that there's a bigger problem lurking in the background. It often happens that the core problem is that this Prospect doesn't really have the buying authority that he claimed to have, and is embarrassed now to admit it.

Your asking, Is there someone else who should be sitting in with us? gives him a face-saving way of admitting—without really admitting—that the boss actually needs to sign off on this purchase.

7. The ultimate probe: "What can we do to make this sale happen?"

Sometimes the simplest probe is the best: skip over the objection and simply ask something to the effect, "What can we do to make this sale happen?"

Or, alternately, ask, "How could we change the product mix (or the offer, or whatever is relevant in this case) to make it more helpful to you?"

What the Prospect tells you may open up the sale, particularly if what she says that will make the sale happen is within your power to bring about.

But even if it isn't something you can change, then at least the response to that open-ended probe will unblock both your own and the Prospect's thinking, opening the way for a deal to be struck.

Worst case: Even if you can't work out a sale at this point, what the Prospect tells you can at least serve as practical feedback that can help you reshape your product or service for the future, or reshape the terms of the offer (such as payment terms, and the like).

Summary: Responding to objections and questions

1. In many cases, what seems to be an objection is actually a question in disguise. Conversely, what seems to be a question may actually be an objection.

2. You can lose the sale if you don't find out what the customer is thinking behind the words.

3. When you hear no, or when you hear an objection, don't fold. Find what the real concern is, then turn it around and use that as a selling point.

4. Objections and questions can provide the key to the sale, provided you are able to get through assumptions and facades to explore the real meaning.

5. The basic approach in responding to objections and questions: Explore, Listen Well, Restate (if appropriate), Respond, then Move on.

6. Rule of thumb: if, when you explore an objection, you find that the Prospect's reasons keeps shifting, or the Prospect keeps raising additional objections, that indicates that you have not yet cut to the core of the real concern.

7. The ultimate probe: "What can we do to make this sale happen?"

Step 16: AFTER THE SALE: CUSTOMER CARE, AND FOLLOW-UP

On one level, customers are buying your product or professional services.

But on another level, equally important, they also expect that part of the deal is your consistent personal follow-up to ensure that all goes well.

If you fail to provide this follow-up care, you convert what could have been profitable on-going relationships with repeat business and lucrative referrals into single dead-ended sales.

Follow-Up Letters

By granting time for a meeting, the Prospect is doing you a favor. (At least, that's how the Prospect typically perceives it.)

It's good professional business practice to send a short follow-up letter after the sales call as a way of repaying that courtesy.

Another thank-you note is in order after the contract has been signed, to say thanks for the business.

*However, your courtesy note is **not just** a courtesy.* It's also an excellent way of re-selling the points you made earlier, or of re-opening closed doors.

You can merge the Prospect's name and address from a data base with a basic letter. Most of the letter will be standard, though you can customize it to reflect the special points touched on in your face-to-face meeting.

How and what to say

In your follow-up letter, begin by thanking the Prospect for taking time out from a busy schedule to meet with you.

Then briefly summarize your discussions about the client's needs and how your product can fill those needs, cost-effectively.

If appropriate, summarize what follow-up actions had been agreed-upon (such as that you would do some research and then get back to the Prospect with the answers.) Respond to any questions that were raised.

It's essential to take notes during, or just following, each sales call. Otherwise, by the end of the day, all of the calls will have blurred, and you'll have very little idea of what you agreed upon with each Prospects.

As with any other correspondence you send, be sure to paper-clip your business card to the letter: even if you have already handed out a couple of cards, they may have been lost. Business cards are cheap, so use them freely.

Tip: when you come to write your follow-up letter, you'll need to have the Prospect's precise address, and correct spelling of her name, so be sure to get her business card while you're on the premises.

Here's a model letter you can adapt to your situation:

YOUR LETTERHEAD

Date

Ms. Janice Decision-Maker
President
Prospect Products
1 Pleasant St.
Pleasantville

Dear Ms. Decision-Maker:

Newbie's Guide to Selling Face-to-Face

I appreciate your investing the time to meet with me yesterday, and discuss some of the needs you anticipate this year. These included:

- Desire to increase output in the production unit by 20%.

- Intention to hold staffing level steady during this time.

- Corporate objective of holding capital investments to a minimum.

How the GEM 2000 will fill those needs

As I explained in our meeting, the GEM 2000 will assist in meeting these needs:

- Our customer surveys show that installation of the GEM 2000 has assisted in increasing production output by an average of 15%. Further, its low maintenance requirements allow it to be operated with 11% less down-time, meaning that it could be operated longer hours, achieving the goal of a 20% increase.

- The GEM 2000 can be operated by one person, instead of the three staff-members needed by most competing machines. This alone would allow you to reduce staffing by two persons, or to assign them to other duties.

- We do have a lease program available, which would mean the GEM 2000 could be in place with no capital investment necessary on the part of Prospect Products.

Presentation of our cost proposal

Overall, installation of the GEM 2000 will mean high output with significantly lowered cost. As we agreed, I will prepare a cost proposal for the GEM 2000 and present it to you on Thursday August 12, at 11 A.M. at your office.

Again, thank you for the time and interest, and I look forward to Prospect Products joining our client list.

Sincerely,

J. Seller

Michael McGaulley

Follow-up customer care calls

In the months and years after a customer has bought from you, it's good business courtesy to keep in touch through occasional customer care calls when you check to make sure things are working as promised, with no problems.

For the reasons we covered earlier, cold-calling—that is, just dropping in on offices—is usually not a productive use of your time in making initial calls, but it can be very appropriate for follow-up customer care calls.

Even if the Prospect is unable to see you, at least you can accomplish your customer care purpose by appearing and showing interest. The secretary or receptionist will inform the Prospect that you have been there.

By showing this kind of interest, you demonstrate your resolve to make sure that the buyer is satisfied. That puts you in an excellent position for gaining repeat business from this customer and from other Prospects he refers on the basis of your superior performance.

Follow-up customer care calls usually tend to be short, and you'll have a good chance of getting in, even without an appointment.

Even if the secretary is unable to fit you in with the boss, leave your business card, so the Prospect knows that you cared enough to drop by to check on things. Next time, you'll probably get put through at once.

A concluding note

Back at the start of this book, I quoted a couple of wise sayings. **The first:**

"First drafts are for getting it down on paper; later drafts are for getting it perfect."

We could rephrase that, First drafts of a sales approach are for getting started; later drafts are for getting it good.

And the other . . .

"The perfect is the greatest enemy of the good-enough."

My point was, Yes, do read this book; yes, do think through how you will apply the lessons contained.

But then, soon, get your feet wet. Don't just think about selling, actually go out and try it. (At least make some of the calls for seeking advice, as we discussed in the Preface to this book.)

Once you have taken those first steps and actually gone face-to-face, then you'll have a much better sense of what "the market" (that is, the real world), thinks about your proposal. At that point, you can pause (briefly!) and rethink.

At that point, you'll also have a better sense of what you need to do in refining your sales approach, or in sharpening your sales skills.

With best wishes,

Michael McGaulley   www.Sales-Training-Source.com

ABOUT THE AUTHOR / OTHER BOOKS

The books in the two series described here flow from my experience first as a lawyer, then a management consultant working with companies that included Xerox in the United States, Canada and Europe; Kodak; Sylvania; Bank of America; Motorola, and others.

Part of my work involved analyzing the key skills and competencies that make the difference between top-performing managers, sales people and sales managers, then developing training programs, guides, and job-aids to teach these skills to new trainees and those who had been working below their full potential. The books in this series draw from that experience.

Books in the SMALL BUSINESS SALES HOW-TO SERIES:

These first two books were developed primarily for people new to sales. The *NEWBIE'S GUIDE* is a quick handbook; *TUTORIALS* is a longer, more hands-on self-instructional course.

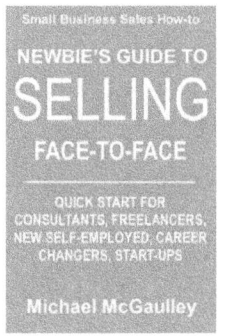

NEWBIE'S GUIDE TO SELLING-FACE-TO-FACE is a short, to-the-point handbook focusing on the need-to-know for people getting started in the process of finding prospects and making face-to-face sales calls.

It's especially targeted to the needs of career-changers and people going off on their own, or looking for a new job or a new field—such as consultants, free-agents, or independent contractors.

Michael McGaulley

SELLING 101 is directed to more experienced salespeople who want access the kind of sales training courses I developed for major marketing firms including Xerox, Kodak, and others. (The 101 title was chosen by the original publisher I think 201 or 301 would have been a better fit, but they were the publisher, and I was only the author!)

This **SALES TRAINING WORKSHOP-LEADER GUIDE** is the instructor's guide for the text, *Selling 101: Consultative Selling Skills.*

Who this sales training workshop--leader guide is intended for

Sales managers looking for materials for sales team meetings.

Instructors in new entrepreneur training workshops.

Instructors in community colleges or similar job-training programs

What this sales training workshop - leader guide provides

The 14 Modules in the Workshop Leader Guide track the coverage in **SELLING 101**, linking to specific pages for ease in linking across.

A chart at the start of each Module provides a succinct overview of what that module is about, suggested time to allow, as well as materials and set-up.

The content within the modules guide the instructor or leader through clearly-marked sections, such as

Newbie's Guide to Selling Face-to-Face

- Overview and set context,
- Lead discussion,
- Explain,
- Pair trainees for one-on-one role plays,
- Conduct whole-group debriefing, and,
- Wrap-up and overview the next module.

Pre-class assignments for each module are provided, which the workshop leader can copy and pass out in advance. These guide the trainee on the reading assignment (chapters or sections from the course text, *Selling 101*), as well as other preparation, such as discussions and role-play exercises to prepare for.

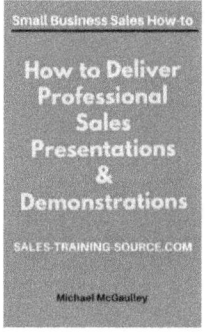

HOW TO DELIVER PROFESSIONAL SALES PRESENTATIONS AND DEMONSTRATIONS covers the practical how-to of presenting or demonstrating in front of the prospect, as well as the very important matter of reading (and sending) non-verbal messages. It also addresses the essential point that demonstrations, presentations, proposals, free-trials, discounts and other special deals are "proof sources," given for a specific, defined purpose, agreed-upon in advance with the prospective buyer.

Michael McGaulley

CAREER SAVVY PEOPLE SKILLS SERIES

Book #1

Am I Asking the Right Questions? provides the tools for, among many others, looking through to what's really going on in situations, for spotting the "real rules", for focusing on what in fact does matter, for staying out of unnecessary confrontations.

"You've got to be aware of the games that are being played. You don't have to play the games yourself, but you do need to recognize when they are being played against you."

Book #2

When you ask a question, *most* of the time, *most* people will do their best to tell the truth. But not always. Sometimes simply to ask a question is to give the game away because it alerts the other person to what you're really after, and hence raises a flag on what they may want to fudge, avoid, or distort. (Or even tell a fib!) **Mental Pickpocketing** introduces you to an array of methods of getting to the truth without *seeming* to ask questions.

Book #3

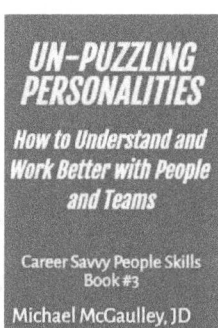

Emotional intelligence is recognized as a particularly valuable asset in today's career world. **Un-Puzzling Personalities** is based on the system developed by Carl Jung, and includes self-instructional tutorials including mini-cases, as well as application checklists and worksheets.

The system is clear and helpful in taking a fresh look at oneself, as well as in understanding how others perceive and react in different ways to events and communications.

Michael McGaulley

Legal and copyright notices continued from the front of this book

Copyright © 2009-2021, Michael McGaulley.

All rights reserved. Champlain House Media.

No part of this book, whether delivered electronically (e-book) or in conventional paper form (p-book), may be reproduced or transmitted in any form by any means graphic, electronic, or mechanical without the written permission from the author, Michael McGaulley, the publisher, or affiliated companies.

No part of this book, whether delivered electronically (e-book) or in conventional paper form (p-book), may be reproduced or transmitted in any form by any means graphic, electronic, or mechanical without the written permission from the author, Michael McGaulley, the publisher, or affiliated companies. This book is intellectual property. No part of this publication may be stored in a retrieval system, transmitted or reproduced in any way, including but not limited to digital copying and printing without the prior agreement and written permission of the author and publisher.

Necessary legal disclaimers, provisos, and such

The contents of this book reflect the author's views acquired through experience in the areas addressed. The author is not engaged in rendering any legal, financial or accounting advice. Business customs, courtesies, and legal implications vary with the context, and with geographic region or country. Accordingly, anyone reading this material should not rely totally on the contents herein, and should seek the advice of others. The author has made his best effort to ensure that this is a helpful and informative manual. The contents are recommendations only, and the author cannot take responsibility for loss or action to any individual or corporation acting, or not acting, as a result of the material presented here.

Newbie's Guide to Selling Face-to-Face

While the information contained within the pages of this electronic book, other related books and e-books, and the related web-site, is periodically updated, no guarantee is given that the information provided is correct, complete, and/or up-to-date.

The materials contained in this e-book and related website are provided for general information purposes only and do not constitute legal or other professional advice on any subject matter. Neither the author nor publisher accept any responsibility for any loss which may arise from reliance on information contained in this book or related website.

Some links within this e-book or related website may lead to other websites, including those operated and maintained by third parties. The author and publisher of this e-book include these links solely as a convenience to you, and the presence of such a link does not imply a responsibility for the linked site or an endorsement of the linked site, its operator, or its contents.

The publisher and author accept no liability whatsoever for any losses or damages caused or alleged to be caused, directly or indirectly, by utilization of any information contained herein, or obtained from any of the persons or entities herein above.

This book and related website and its contents are provided "AS IS" without warranty of any kind, either express or implied, including, but not limited to, the implied warranties of merchantability, fitness for a particular purpose, or non-infringement.

If you, or any other reader, do not agree to these policies as noted above, please do not use these materials or any services offered herein.

Your use of these materials indicates acceptance of these policies.

This book is intellectual property. No part of this publication may be stored in a retrieval system, transmitted or reproduced in any way, including but not limited to digital copying and printing without the prior agreement and written permission of the author and publisher.

www.ingramcontent.com/pod-product-compliance
Lightning Source LLC
Chambersburg PA
CBHW071439180526
45170CB00001B/389